An Analysis of

Sir Philip Sidney's

The Defence of Poesy

Liam Haydon

Published by Macat International Ltd
24:13 Coda Centre, 189 Munster Road, London SW6 6AW.

Distributed exclusively by Routledge
2 Park Square, Milton Park, Abingdon, Oxon OX14 4RN
711 Third Avenue, New York, NY 10017, USA

Routledge is an imprint of the Taylor & Francis Group, an informa business

Printed by CPI Group (UK) Ltd, Croydon CRO 4YY

www.macat.com
info@macat.com

Cataloguing in Publication Data
A catalogue record for this book is available from the British Library.
Library of Congress Cataloguing-in-Publication Data is available upon request.
Cover illustration: Capucine Deslouis

ISBN 978-1-912453-58-0 (hardback)
ISBN 978-1-912453-13-9 (paperback)
ISBN 978-1-912453-28-3 (e-book)

Notice
The information in this book is designed to orientate readers of the work under analysis,
to elucidate and contextualise its key ideas and themes, and to aid in the development
of critical thinking skills. It is not meant to be used, nor should it be used, as a
substitute for original thinking or in place of original writing or research. References and
notes are provided for informational purposes and their presence does not constitute
endorsement of the information or opinions therein. This book is presented solely for
educational purposes. It is sold on the understanding that the publisher is not engaged
to provide any scholarly advice. The publisher has made every effort to ensure that
this book is accurate and up-to-date, but makes no warranties or representations with
regard to the completeness or reliability of the information it contains. The information
and the opinions provided herein are not guaranteed or warranted to produce particular
results and may not be suitable for students of every ability. The publisher shall not be
liable for any loss, damage or disruption arising from any errors or omissions, or from
the use of this book, including, but not limited to, special, incidental, consequential or
other damages caused, or alleged to have been caused, directly or indirectly, by the
information contained within.

CONTENTS

WAYS IN TO THE TEXT

Who Was Sir Philip Sidney?   9
What Does *The Defence of Poesy* Say?   10
Why Does *The Defence of Poesy* Matter?   11

SECTION 1: INFLUENCES

Module 1: The Author and the Historical Context   14
Module 2: Academic Context   18
Module 3: The Problem   22
Module 4: The Author's Contribution   26

SECTION 2: IDEAS

Module 5: Main Ideas   31
Module 6: Secondary Ideas   35
Module 7: Achievement   39
Module 8: Place in the Author's Work   43

SECTION 3: IMPACT

Module 9: The First Responses   48
Module 10: The Evolving Debate   52
Module 11: Impact and Influence Today   56
Module 12: Where Next?   60

Glossary of Terms   65
People Mentioned in the Text   69
Works Cited   76

THE MACAT LIBRARY

The Macat Library is a series of unique academic explorations of seminal works in the humanities and social sciences – books and papers that have had a significant and widely recognised impact on their disciplines. It has been created to serve as much more than just a summary of what lies between the covers of a great book. It illuminates and explores the influences on, ideas of, and impact of that book. Our goal is to offer a learning resource that encourages critical thinking and fosters a better, deeper understanding of important ideas.

Each publication is divided into three Sections: Influences, Ideas, and Impact. Each Section has four Modules. These explore every important facet of the work, and the responses to it.

This Section-Module structure makes a Macat Library book easy to use, but it has another important feature. Because each Macat book is written to the same format, it is possible (and encouraged!) to cross-reference multiple Macat books along the same lines of inquiry or research. This allows the reader to open up interesting interdisciplinary pathways.

To further aid your reading, lists of glossary terms and people mentioned are included at the end of this book (these are indicated by an asterisk [*] throughout) – as well as a list of works cited.

Macat has worked with the University of Cambridge to identify the elements of critical thinking and understand the ways in which six different skills combine to enable effective thinking.
Three allow us to fully understand a problem; three more give us the tools to solve it. Together, these six skills make up the **PACIER** model of critical thinking. They are:

ANALYSIS – understanding how an argument is built
EVALUATION – exploring the strengths and weaknesses of an argument
INTERPRETATION – understanding issues of meaning

CREATIVE THINKING – coming up with new ideas and fresh connections
PROBLEM-SOLVING – producing strong solutions
REASONING – creating strong arguments

To find out more, visit **WWW.MACAT.COM.**

CRITICAL THINKING AND *THE DEFENCE OF POESY*

Primary critical thinking skill: REASONING
Secondary critical thinking skill: CREATIVE THINKING

Though Sidney's text is about the emotional power of writing, he constructs his argument in a rational, highly structured form. He begins with a general introduction (or *exordium*); states the facts that support poetry's status (*narration*); establishes his main argument (or *proposition*), that poetry is morally effective because it is delightful; *divides* poetry up into genres which are then used as *confirmation* of his proposition; *refutes* the case made against poetry, by considering the counter-arguments (real and potential) which had been made against the position by both classical and contemporary authors; and finally comes to a *conclusion* by restating the value of poetry, and considering how it is not practiced in England and in the English language.

These features are still the basis of persuasive writing today. Sidney shows how carefully he has evaluated his case, encouraging his reader to do the same—if his reasoning is correct, then logically his defense of poetry must have been successful. The careful structure is actually necessary for the creative argument Sidney is making. He is combining a range of intellectual materials, across a number of languages and intellectual traditions, to create a history of, and an imagined future for, poetry. Whether that is finding poetry in the work of the philosophers, or analyzing the mingling of comedy and tragedy, Sidney's connections help to redefine poetry as a vital part of human endeavor.

ABOUT THE AUTHOR OF THE ORIGINAL WORK

Sir Philip Sidney was born into a noble family in 1554. He became one of the best-known public figures of the Elizabethan age–known for his dashing adventures overseas in service of the crown, for poems that included the sonnet sequence *Astrophil and Stella*, and for his great personal charm and wit. When he died in 1586, killed by gangrene that infected a bullet wound received in battle in the Netherlands, he received the grandest funeral accorded to any Englishman in history, other than a king or queen, until that of Winston Churchill. *The Defence of Poesy* was his only critical work.

ABOUT THE AUTHOR OF THE ANALYSIS

Liam Haydon was educated at Queen's University Belfast and the University of Manchester, where he wrote a PhD on Milton's *Paradise Lost*. He is currently a postdoctoral scholar at the Centre for the Political Economies of International Commerce at the University of Kent. His work focuses on the cultural history of the seventeenth century, exploring connections between the corporation, economic ideology, and literature.

ABOUT MACAT

GREAT WORKS FOR CRITICAL THINKING

Macat is focused on making the ideas of the world's great thinkers accessible and comprehensible to everybody, everywhere, in ways that promote the development of enhanced critical thinking skills.

It works with leading academics from the world's top universities to produce new analyses that focus on the ideas and the impact of the most influential works ever written across a wide variety of academic disciplines. Each of the works that sit at the heart of its growing library is an enduring example of great thinking. But by setting them in context – and looking at the influences that shaped their authors, as well as the responses they provoked – Macat encourages readers to look at these classics and game-changers with fresh eyes. Readers learn to think, engage and challenge their ideas, rather than simply accepting them.

'Macat offers an amazing first-of-its-kind tool for interdisciplinary learning and research. Its focus on works that transformed their disciplines and its rigorous approach, drawing on the world's leading experts and educational institutions, opens up a world-class education to anyone.'

Andreas Schleicher,
Director for Education and Skills, Organisation for Economic Co-operation and Development

'Macat is taking on some of the major challenges in university education … They have drawn together a strong team of active academics who are producing teaching materials that are novel in the breadth of their approach.'

Prof Lord Broers,
former Vice-Chancellor of the University of Cambridge

'The Macat vision is exceptionally exciting. It focuses upon new modes of learning which analyse and explain seminal texts which have profoundly influenced world thinking and so social and economic development. It promotes the kind of critical thinking which is essential for any society and economy. This is the learning of the future.'

Rt Hon Charles Clarke, former UK Secretary of State for Education

'The Macat analyses provide immediate access to the critical conversation surrounding the books that have shaped their respective discipline, which will make them an invaluable resource to all of those, students and teachers, working in the field.'

Professor William Tronzo, University of California at San Diego

WAYS IN TO THE TEXT

KEY POINTS

- Sir Philip Sidney was a prominent courtier, diplomat, soldier and poet.
- *The Defence of Poesy* argues that poetry offers a uniquely effective way to promote virtuous action in the reader.
- *The Defence* is a powerful defense of the humanities generally, not just of poetry, and a wonderful example of persuasive writing.

Who Was Sir Philip Sidney?

Sir Philip Sidney was born in 1554 at Penshurst, a country house in Kent, into a family with important connections in the English nobility and the royal family. He was trained in the law, and finished his education by travelling across Europe. As a result of his experiences, he was tasked with a number of important diplomatic missions, as well as command of English troops on the continent. It was on one of these missions, in the Netherlands in 1586, that he received the wound that would kill him.

Sidney's career as a poet was secondary to his military and political ambitions, and he left much of his work unfinished and unprinted (it did circulate in manuscript form). Nonetheless, his work was hugely influential in the century after his death; both his pastoral* work *Arcadia* and the sonnet sequence *Astrophil and Stella* were imitated and borrowed from liberally by 17th-century figures. Charles I* even recited Pamela's prayer from the *Arcadia* on his way to be executed, which Milton* attacked as a profanity in his anti-monarchical text *Eikonoklastes*: "a prayer stolen word for word from the mouth of a heathen fiction ... the vain amatorious poem of Sir Philip Sidney's *Arcadia*."[1] As with many Renaissance* authors, Sidney's literary style (full of allusions to classical texts, deliberately witty and self-conscious) fell out of favor in the 18th century, which saw the rise of the novel and increasingly realist writing.

What Does *The Defence of Poesy* Say?

The Defence of Poesy provides a passionate yet scholarly argument that "poetry" (by which Sidney, who wrote well before the development of the modern novel, in fact meant poetry, drama and anything else that had a ⟨literary⟩ quality such as history, philosophy or even scripture) is an important moral and intellectual pursuit. Sidney argues that poetry is the best kind of writing because it provides a delightful example of moral behavior, and in so doing encourages the reader to emulate the figures it describes. The delightfulness is the key feature which sets poetry apart from the other types of writing Sidney discusses; history and philosophy, he claims, are so dry as to make the reader think they are back in school. While a reader of history or philosophy might be rationally convinced of the correctness of the view put forth in such a text, they would struggle to bring its lessons into their own lives. Poetry, by contrast, works on the rational and emotional level at once—it provides an ideal picture of the way things should, or could be, and because of the emotions it stirs in the reader, encourages them to seek that ideal state in their own life.

By separating poetry from philosophy and history, Sidney opened up a critical space in which literature could be discussed as seriously as other forms of knowledge, rather than dismissed as a distracting or pernicious influence. *The Defence of Poesy* stands as the first major analysis of literature in English, making an intervention into both the ideal state and actual practice of poetry. Even the technical parts of the text add to Sidney's moral message—the discussion of how English poetry might fit to classical meter,* for example, is both a useful guide for writers and a strongly nationalistic pitch from an English poet. The *Defence* was also the first English text to divide poetry into the genres that are familiar to us today, and in doing so set the pattern for literary criticism through the next century, or beyond. It became the model for writing about poetry for the early modern period and later, and is now widely acknowledged as one of the foundational texts of English literary criticism.

As well as establishing a new field of enquiry, Sidney uses the *Defence* to counter an anti-literary movement that had gained traction in England. Writers such as Stephen Gosson* produced treatises explaining why literature, especially drama, was a dangerous influence, because it encouraged its readers to follow bad examples: they are "drawn to vanity by wanton poets."[2] Sidney provides an alternative, positive model of emulation, since the reader he describes is actually led to "virtuous action" by reading poetry.[3] He shows that poetry is (or can be) a serious form that can be both educational and pleasurable. The depth of learning, witty style, and preoccupation with the aesthetics of poetry in the *Defence* made it a key Renaissance text, whose central message endures today.

Why Does *The Defence of Poesy* Matter?

Many of Sidney's key ideas have already been well developed, not least the division of poetry into specific and distinguishable kinds, which was an embryonic version of formalism and genre theory. The text itself, therefore, despite being an important reference point because of its role as origin, has largely been superseded by later critical developments. Sidney's concern with the emotional and instructive elements of poetry are part of a long debate on the response of the reader to a text, and understanding how those views have evolved is useful, albeit not necessary, for students of critical theory today.

Alongside its content, though, the *Defence* is a particularly fine example of how to structure a work of criticism. It is structured as a classical piece of rhetoric–such as a political speech, or the way a lawyer might sum up a court case–setting out its arguments clearly and methodically. It establishes why the question it asks is important, presents a narrative of its own case, imagines and then answers potential counter-arguments, applies its methodology to a current example, and then reaches a conclusion. While today's critical or persuasive writing might not be so rigidly structured, a careful reader of Sidney's text will find the form just as instructive as the content.

Moreover, the central question of the *Defence*—what makes literature so powerful and important?—remains as pressing now as it was in 1595. *The Defence of Poesy* may not be much read today, but it nonetheless engages with a timeless question: What is literature? The closing pages of *The Defence of Poesy* offer a forceful and passionate appeal on behalf of poetry. Sidney contends that "the ever-praiseworthy poesy is full of virtue-breeding delightfulness," that poets are the "first bringers-in of all civility" and "give us all knowledge."[4] The *Defence* still prompts its readers to reflect on their relationship with literature, how it moves them, and why it is so valuable. At a time when public funding for the arts is increasingly coming under attack, we should return to Sidney's closing statement as a powerful reminder of the importance and vitality of literature.

NOTES

1 John Milton, *Eikonoklastes* (1649), in *Complete Prose of John Milton*, ed. Merritt Y. Hughes, 6 vols (New Haven: Yale University Press, 1962), 3:505.

2 Stephen Gosson, *The School of Abuse* (London: 1579), 8.

3 Philip Sidney, *The Defence of Poesy* (1595), in *Sidney's "The Defence of Poesy" and Selected Renaissance Literary Criticism*, ed. Gavin Alexander (London: Penguin, 2004), 13.

4 Sidney, *The Defence of Poesy*, 53.

SECTION 1
INFLUENCES

MODULE 1
THE AUTHOR AND THE
HISTORICAL CONTEXT

KEY POINTS

- *The Defence of Poesy* is one of the earliest and most influential pieces of literary criticism in English.

- Sidney was thoroughly trained in classical literature and rhetoric.

- *The Defence* draws on the ideas circulating in the Renaissance to produce a new kind of text in English.

Why Read This Text?

Sir Philip Sidney's *The Defence of Poesy* was the first major piece of literary criticism in English. Though some figures are used repeatedly as examples, it did not focus on particular authors, instead offering a thoughtful criticism of literature as a whole: what is the purpose of poetic writing? How does it benefit its readers? And how does it benefit society? Sidney's answer was that poetry was a way of revealing essential truths about society, or moral virtue, in a way that encouraged readers to assimilate them into their own lives. Unlike histories, sermons, or other moralizing writing, "poesy" (i.e. literature) was able to demonstrate virtue in a way that was highly enjoyable, and so more convincing and effective than texts which simply discussed virtue and lectured the reader.

The *Defence* became an important tool for poets and literary critics in the 17th century (the two categories often overlapped at the time, as in Sidney's own case). The questions it asks of literature are still asked today: recent cuts to education once more ask the humanities to explain what value they have. The powerful and persuasive language

> **❝** Now therein of all sciences (I speak still of human, and according to the human conceit) is our poet the monarch. For he doth not only show the way, but giveth so sweet a prospect into the way as will entice any man to enter into it. **❞**
>
> Sidney, *Defence of Poesy*

of the *Defence* is a model answer against such criticism. Though questions about the morality of literature have now largely migrated to other types of cultural production (such as films or television), Sidney's insistence on the positively transformative power of representations, in any form, still resonates.

Author's Life
Sir Philip Sidney, famous as a courtier,* soldier, and poet, was one of the most prominent figures in Elizabethan* England. He was born in 1554 into an influential and sometimes controversial family: his grandfather, John Dudley, Duke of Northumberland,* had been executed for treason the year before, after trying to put Lady Jane Grey* on the throne instead of Henry VIII's daughter Mary.* Among his godparents was Philip II of Spain,* the husband of Queen Mary. Almost from his birth, courtiers and key political figures surrounded Sidney.

His education, as was common for young noblemen, took him to Gray's Inn* (for training in the law) and then, aged 13, to Christ Church, Oxford, where he probably studied a range of Greek and Latin authors, philosophy and theology. He would also have continued his training, begun in Gray's Inn (if not before), in oratory and debate. One Oxford contemporary described the terrifying experience of being "called to debate *ex tempore* [unplanned or impromptu] with the matchless Sir Ph Sidney."[1] Even at an early age,

Sidney was demonstrating the wit, education and ability that would later characterize *The Defence of Poesy*.

A key part of all Sidney's education was the study of disputation, or rhetorical training, and this background clearly informs the precisely structured, witty and persuasive *Defence of Poesy*. Furthermore, the title of the piece, as well as the rhetorical structure, establishes the text within the humanist tradition in which "defenses" of theoretical or philosophical subjects were common, in order to demonstrate the learning of the author as well as persuade and encourage the readers.

Author's Background

The Defence of Poesy emerges from the Renaissance, a cultural moment in which the great texts and ideas of classical antiquity were rediscovered and re-examined. This was not just a literary phenomenon, though written texts were crucial; many disciplines were revived or invented in this period, such as art, architecture, cartography, history, philosophy and astronomy. Renaissance thinkers absorbed, questioned and appropriated the newly available texts of classical antiquity, not simply spreading the knowledge of these classic texts but building on them, refining them, and using them as starting points for new inventions and insights.

Sidney's work, then, is in one sense not "original"; like many Renaissance writings, it is a reworking and a development of old ideas, albeit collected together and placed in a new context. In many ways it is a development (and refutation) of classical ideas on poetry, especially those of Plato,* Aristotle* and Horace.* These ideas had been developed by Italian writers in the early part of the 16th century, and Sidney follows their preference for setting up precise rules for, and "kinds" (genres) of, poetry. However, Sidney goes further than Aristotle's relatively simple division into "tragedy", "comedy" and "lyric", labeling precise genres such as "heroic", "pastoral" and "satiric."[2] *The Defence of Poesy* insightfully and skillfully combines these earlier texts to produce a single, rhetorical, piece. Sidney's text is a highly learned consideration of the formal and moral qualities of poetry, and was one of the first attempts to perform this analysis in English.

NOTES

1   Richard Carew, *Survey of Cornwall* (1602), fol. 102v.

2   Philip Sidney, *The Defence of Poesy*, (1595), in *Sidney's "The Defence of Poesy" and Selected Renaissance Literary Criticism*, ed. Gavin Alexander (London: Penguin, 2004), 11.

ACADEMIC CONTEXT

KEY POINTS

- The work is partly a response to Plato's attack on poets.
- The *Defence* draws on the humanist* tradition which places emphasis on learning.
- Sidney combines the ideas and writings of classic thinkers on literature.

The Work in Its Context

Philip Sidney's *The Defence of Poesy* emerges out of the Renaissance, a period of intellectual development across continental Europe fueled by the rediscovery of classical texts, and a new spirit of scholarly enquiry dedicated to reassessing and updating those ancient writers. The Renaissance was a period when many "new" ideas circulated, but these were often old ideas which had been forgotten, or overlooked; usually Renaissance thinkers "worked by adapting old forms or imparting to them a new spirit," partly because of a belief that the great forms and ideas of classical antiquity had been degraded over subsequent centuries.[1]

Renaissance scholars frequently combined knowledge across what we would now consider separate areas of inquiry—Philip Sidney himself was trained in the law, was familiar with international politics and military strategy, as well as being an accomplished poet. In this, too, they were following classical precedent, since one of the major pieces of what we would now call literary criticism was found in Plato's *Republic*, a political tract which discussed the design of an ideal community. In the *Republic*, Plato had argued that his community ought to exclude poets (or at least most poets), because they tell "false

> ❝ Plato, banishing the abuse, not the thing – not banishing it, but giving due honour to it – shall be our patron and not our adversary. ❞
>
> Sidney, *Defence of Poesy*

stories." The risk of these fables, myths, or lies is that "[young] people can't distinguish the allegorical from the non-allegorical, and what enters the mind at that age tends to become indelible."[2]

Plato's charge—that poets are liars and their untruths, however well-intentioned, are de facto dangerous because they spread false ideas or create an excess of emotion—was answered by Aristotle in his *Poetics*. He discussed Plato's "charge of not being true" and noted that "one can say 'But perhaps it is as it should be'."[3] That is, poetry can, through its imaginative qualities, suggest a better world to its audience, just as Plato's philosophy did. Until the Renaissance, this debate over truth and emotion was the standard form of literary criticism.

Overview of the Field

The *Defence* draws on a number of schools of thought established during the Renaissance, but none more than the humanism* that was developed within continental Europe. Humanism was a diverse and multifaceted intellectual movement that emphasized the potential of the individual, and stressed the value of education, particularly in Classics and in critical thinking. *The Defence of Poesy* expresses this in its description of learning, which will "draw us to so high a perfection as our degenerate souls, made worse by their clayey lodgings, can be capable of."[4] The treatise is concerned both with the logical and the rhetorical or literary strands of humanism; it analyses the different kinds of poetry that exist in a careful, precise manner, but simultaneously exalts the power of poetry to produce emotion in the reader far beyond the dry precision of history or philosophy.

In doing so, *The Defence of Poesy* marks the beginning of intellectual engagement with the practice of writing (in England). Nothing like it had been attempted before; the only contemporary text to examine poetry, George Puttenham's* *Art of English Poesy,* is much more concerned with technical features of poetry such as meter than with the art of poetry in general.[5]

Academic Influences

Sidney's classical education clearly influences the content, as well as the rhetorical form of the *Defence*. The ideas of *The Defence of Poesy* are rarely, if ever, completely original to Sidney, but are usually taken from classical or continental texts on the theme of poetry. The key sources for the *Defence* are classical texts rediscovered (or reinterpreted) in the Renaissance, such as Plato's *Republic,* or Aristotle's *Poetics.* The originality of the *Defence,* then, comes in the combination of these sources in English—more than merely translating, Sidney combines, contrasts and critically examines these source materials to construct his own argument (albeit following Aristotle) for the power of poetry. The *Defence* is a seminal text precisely because it performs this *bricolage,** which was only possible because of Sidney's extensive classical education.

The other key influence on *The Defence of Poesy* is the idea of courtliness. Sidney served at the court of Elizabeth, and was regarded by those around him, and on the continent, as a talented and entertaining member of the queen's entourage. A crucial part of courtly life was to entertain the monarch, often in order to gain personal advancement. Sidney, for example, produced pastoral plays for the queen in order to secure a place on a diplomatic trip to the Netherlands in 1578. In his guide to being a courtier, Castiglione* instructs the aspiring courtier to "much exercise himself in poets, and no less in Orators", since it is through these skills that a monarch will be both pleased ad persuaded.[6] The *Defence* captures this duality in its key phrase "to instruct and delight";[7] in many ways, the moral arguments for poetry outlined by Sidney also serve as a self-justification for the courtly practice of poetic production.

NOTES

1   Alistair Fowler, "The Formation of Genres in the Renaissance and After", *New Literary History* 34.2 (2003) 185-200 (185).

2   Plato, *Republic*, in *Classical Literary Criticism*, ed. D.A. Russell and Michael Winterbottom (Oxford: Oxford University Press, 1998), 15-6.

3   Aristotle, *Poetics*, in *Classical Literary Criticism*, 85.

4   Philip Sidney, *The Defence of Poesy*, in *Sidney's "The Defence of Poesy" and Selected Renaissance Literary Criticism*, ed. Gavin Alexander (London: Penguin, 2004), 12.

5   George Puttenham, *The Art of English Poesy* (1589), in *Sidney's "The Defence of Poesy" and Selected Renaissance Literary Criticism*, ed. Gavin Alexander (London: Penguin, 2004).

6   Baldassare Castiglione, *The Courtier of Count Baldessar Castilio Divided into Four Books*, trans. Thomas Hoby (1561), sig. H4r.

7   Sidney, *The Defence of Poesy*, 10.

MODULE 3
THE PROBLEM

KEY POINTS

- Sidney asks the most fundamental question of all criticism: why is literature special?

- This question was not original to Sidney, but it had renewed force when he was writing.

- Sidney mainly looks back to the classics, but also includes a range of contemporary writers on poetry.

Core Question

At the heart of Philip Sidney's *The Defence of Poesy* lies one of the most fundamental questions in literary criticism: what makes poetry (that is, literature) important, especially in comparison to other modes of writing? This question, in one form or another, has been asked since classical antiquity, and Sidney follows the work of Plato and Aristotle in examining the power of writing to move its audience, and whether it is possible for poetry to be a good example to a populace.

More specifically to the *Defence*, the question serves as a justification for Sidney's own career. He was himself a poet, and this, he claims, gives him "just cause to make a pitiful defense of poor poetry."[1] Since the *Defence* claims that poetry is a valuable tool for education, it is implicitly an argument in support of Sidney's own poetry. This justification was especially pressing when the *Defence* was written, as literary production (especially drama) was increasingly coming under attack for promoting vices such as idleness or immodesty. In a famous passage, George Stubbs wrote that literature mixes "scurrility with divinity" and tended "to the dishonor of God and nourishing of vice."[2] For this reason, Sidney's focus on the importance of literature comes in

> ❝ [The] poet is of all other the most ancient orator, as he that by good and pleasant persuasions first reduced the wild and beastly people into public societies and civility of life, insinuating unto them under fictions with sweet and colored speeches many wholesome lessons and doctrines. ❞
>
> George Puttenham, *The Art of English Poesy*

the form of the linked question, "can poetry be a moral (rather than immoral) force?"

The Participants

The question of the value of poetry was not original to Sidney. It had its source in the classical texts he references, though it had not been discussed in English, apart from by Sidney's older contemporary, George Puttenham, in his manuscript text *The Art of English Poesy*. Like Sidney, Puttenham placed value on the instructive qualities of poetry. However, he focused not on the logical or rhetorical justifications of this position, but on the process by which "good" poetry might be achieved. Consequently, Puttenham's work focused on giving the reader metrical and linguistic guidelines for their own poetry. Counterintuitively, his theoretical intervention into the field is to argue that the point of these rules is to be hidden from the reader, since a poet "will be more commended for his natural eloquence than for his artificial, and more for his artificial well dissembled" (that is, hidden).[3]

Sidney, conversely, seeks to investigate the issue of the value of poetry, which Puttenham takes for granted. To answer the question, Sidney adopts the position of an orator; that is, someone speaking for the public good, as defined by the Roman orator Cicero* in *De Optimo Genere Oratorum* [*On the Ideal Orator*] and adopted widely in the Renaissance as a model for both public life and literary production.[4] Thomas Wilson's* *Art of Rhetoric* was an influential reworking of Cicero's text, and it was an important model for Sidney. Wilson argues that rhetoric is for "such matters as may largely be expounded [discussed]" and that its three linked purposes are "to teach, to delight, and to persuade." For Wilson, and his Renaissance contemporaries, oratory follows a specific pattern that sets out the question under discussion, marshals evidence, deals with counter-arguments and reaches a conclusion.[5]

The Contemporary Debate

Like many Renaissance writers, Sidney establishes his own critical terrain by returning to the questions and debates of classical antiquity. *The Defence of Poesy* is really a defense against Plato, who banished poets from his ideal state on the grounds that they imperfectly copy the real world, without any understanding of it: "[the poet] is an image-maker, far removed indeed from the truth."[6] Sidney's defense is in large part (though not exclusively) a reworking of Aristotle's response to Plato's *Republic* in his *Poetics*. Sidney's argument that poetry is "an art of imitation," with the goal "to teach and delight,"[7] is based closely on Aristotle's suggestion that poetry treats of "people better than are found in the world", and so encourages us to emulate them.[8] Sidney directly quotes Aristotle's concept of *mimesis* [imitation] as the influence for his thinking here; though he does develop Aristotle's arguments towards a much clearer refutation of Plato than is found in the *Poetics*, as well as a more nuanced examination of genre, the *Defence* largely follows Aristotle in its understanding of what poetry is, and what it is for.

The Defence of Poesy has much in common with contemporary European texts, most of which were also responses to Plato's attack on poetry. In his introduction to the *Defence*, Geoffrey Shepherd lists a variety of English and European authors as possible sources who are unacknowledged in the text of the *Defence* itself, but notes that "[scholarly] opinion is sharply divided as to exactly how well he knew these writers' works, and how important they were to him."[9] Sidney certainly had the opportunity to read these (and other) texts, though we will probably never be entirely sure which he had read, and which he had in mind while composing the *Defence*. What can be said for certain is that the *Defence* reflects an increasing Renaissance concern with the form and value of literature: Sidney's text does not necessarily ask these questions anew, but brings together and summarizes thinking on this topic.

NOTES

1   Philip Sidney, *The Defence of Poesy*, in *Sidney's "The Defence of Poesy" and Selected Renaissance Literary Criticism*, ed. Gavin Alexander (London: Penguin, 2004), 4, 16.

2   George Stubbs, *The Anatomy of Abuses* (1583), 88.

3   George Puttenham, *The Art of English Poesy* (1589), in *Sidney's "The Defence of Poesy" and Selected Renaissance Literary Criticism*, ed. Gavin Alexander (London: Penguin, 2004), 202.

4   Marcus Tullius Cicero, *On the Ideal Orator*, translated by James M. May and Jakob Wisse (Oxford: Oxford University Press, 2001).

5   Thomas Wilson, *The Art of Rhetoric* (1553), sig. A1r–A1v.

6   Plato, *Republic*, in *Classical Literary Criticism*, ed. D.A. Russell and Michael Winterbottom (Oxford: Oxford University Press, 1998), 47.

7   Sidney, *The Defence of Poesy*, 10.

8   Aristotle, *Poetics*, in *Classical Literary Criticism,* 70.

9   Philip Sidney, *An Apology for Poetry* [1595] ed. Geoffrey Shepherd (Manchester: Manchester University Press, 2002), 37.

MODULE 4
THE AUTHOR'S CONTRIBUTION

KEY POINTS

- Sidney wanted to defend poetry against the charges that it was a corrupting influence.

- The text is organized as a classical piece of rhetoric, with arguments, counter-arguments, and conclusion.

- Sidney turns classical writings on poetry against contemporary writers who had attacked the value of literature.

Author's Aims

Philip Sidney's main aim in *The Defence of Poesy* is exactly what the title suggests: it is a justification of poetry both as an aesthetic enterprise and as a method of discerning or investigating philosophical truths (such as morality). Sidney intended the work to stand against the anti-poetic tendencies first found in Plato's *Republic* and picked up by the Puritan* (or otherwise anti-theatrical or anti-idleness) groups in Renaissance England and Europe. One typical pamphlet, Stephen Gosson's *The School of Abuse*, was even dedicated to Sidney, and warned of being "drawn to vanity by wanton poets."[1] Sidney's work stands as an important counter to this view, arguing that poetry is an educational force that can "awake the thoughts from the sleep of idleness to embrace honorable enterprises."[2]

Other texts had considered the technical qualities that made poetry "good." Puttenham had done so in English, following a classical tradition dating back to Horace's* *Ars Poetica* and Longinus's* *On the Sublime*. Both of those authors had stressed the need for literature to be a "unified form";[3] that is, an appropriate matching of form to content,

> 66 Poesy, therefore, is an art of imitation, for so Aristotle termeth it in the word *mimesis*, that is to say, a representing, counterfeiting or figuring forth – to speak metaphorically, a speaking picture – with this end: to teach and delight. 99
>
> Sidney, *Defence of Poesy*

mainly with a well-considered, believable plot in the correct poetic meter. Sidney, though he paid some attention to technique, largely focused on poetry in a more abstract way, thinking about the theory, rather than practice of writing. Though this had some precedent in Aristotle and Plato, a sustained analysis in this fashion was unprecedented in contemporary English writing.

As well as being a well-considered text in its own right, *The Defence of Poesy* was (and remains) important because of the career of its author. As a prominent statesman, diplomat, soldier, courtier and poet—a true "Renaissance man"— Sidney was uniquely placed to make a powerful intervention in both the contemporary and classical debates over the value of poetry.

Approach

Sidney justifies his work in two ways: firstly, he gives the anecdote of a similar "demonstration" and "contemplation" of horse-riding, and then notes that poetry "from almost the highest estimation of learning has fallen to be the laughing stock of children."[4] Since poetry ought to be a higher art than riding, he must produce a similarly scholarly defense of the practice. Though this is a return to classic questions, Sidney has added a contemporary urgency by arguing that the attention of witty thinkers has been directed elsewhere, allowing literature to become degraded.

To construct his text, Sidney borrows the structure of classical rhetoric, found in persuasive orations such as that of parliamentary (or senate) debates, or criminal trials. He begins with a general introduction (or *exordium*) on the parallel skill of horse-riding; states the facts that support poetry's status (*narration*) by sketching out a history of poetry and philosophy; establishes his main argument (or *proposition*), that poetry is "an art of imitation [...] to teach and delight", then *divides* poetry up into genres which are shown to be a *confirmation* of his proposition; *refutes* the case made against poetry by historical and contemporary writers; *digresses* into the state of poetry in England; and comes to a *conclusion* by restating the value of poetry.[5] Apart from the digression Sidney follows the rhetorical model precisely, which, for those familiar with the model, makes his text relatively easy to follow; it also helps to give the sense that an irrefutable argument is building throughout the text.

Contribution in Context

In many ways *The Defence of Poesy* exists both in and out of its time; it engages, as so many Renaissance texts do, with the positions and arguments of the rediscovered classics. Sidney begins the treatise by returning to ancient Greek and Roman models of poetry (as well as the biblical psalms).

Throughout, it is largely from those traditions (especially Xenophon,* Homer and Virgil) that Sidney draws his examples. Few contemporary poets are discussed, and it is only in the final pages of the *Defence* that Sidney considers the state of poetry in England. However, it also in many ways reflects the beginnings of Renaissance concern with refashioning these classic texts to reflect contemporary concerns or debates. The *Defence* is probably the first major sustained attempt in English to establish poetic genres, consider form and meter, and query the value of rhyme. It is thus ahead of its time as an early example of the literary production of the early modern period, which was increasingly aware of its own status as high-status "literature."

There was, too, a contemporary debate about the moral qualities of writing. In his educational text *The Schoolmaster,* Roger Ascham* warned his pupils that shops in London were "full of lewd and rude rhymes," because poets did not give enough care to the moral qualities of their poetry, and cared only to be popular.[6] Though the particular controversy to which Sidney was responding had died down by the time the *Defence* was printed, the underlying debate continued, with the closing of the theatres in 1642 on religious grounds being the clearest victory of the anti-literary forces Sidney pitted himself against.

NOTES

1   Stephen Gosson, *The School of Abuse* (London: 1579), 6.

2   Philip Sidney, *The Defence of Poesy,* in *Sidney's "The Defence of Poesy" and Selected Renaissance Literary Criticism,* ed. Gavin Alexander (London: Penguin, 2004), 29.

3   Horace, *The Art of Poetry,* in *Classical Literary Criticism,* ed. D.A. Russell and Michael Winterbottom (Oxford: Oxford University Press, 1998), 98.

4   Sidney, *The Defence of Poesy,* 1-2.

5   Sidney, *The Defence of Poesy,* 10.

6   Roger Ascham, *The Schoolmaster* (London: John Daye, 1570), 60.

SECTION 2
IDEAS

MODULE 5
MAIN IDEAS

KEY POINTS

* Poetry offers a way of thinking about the ideal, not the practical.

* Not only does it show ideal states, it encourages the reader to live up to its examples.

* The *Defence* is itself highly literary, with form and content closely matched.

Key Themes

Philip Sidney introduces his thesis on poetry in *The Defence of Poesy* with an apparently unconnected narrative about learning to ride a horse. He outlines the arguments that his riding teacher made to prove the value of horses, and argues that since poetry is so much more valuable than horses, it deserves a similar rhetorical defense. He asserts that the learning of the ancient world was expressed in poetry, citing a wide and extensive range of poets and scholars from ancient Greece and Rome. These classical precedents are used by Sidney to suggest that poetry can change reality, not just reflect it. He notes that the Greek word for poet comes from "maker," and that "making" allows us to imagine the world in a more ideal state: nature's world, he argues "is brazen [brass], the poets only deliver a golden."[1]

Having established this key idea, *The Defence of Poesy* divides poetry into general and specific kinds. The general kinds are divine, philosophical and didactic (that is, "teaching" or "instructive") poetry. This last category is where Sidney focuses his attention throughout the rest of the treatise, and he divides it into a number of

> 66 Haste, my dear father! ('tis no time to wait)
> And load my shoulders with a willing freight.
> Whate'er befalls, your life shall be my care;
> One death, or one deliverance we will share. 99
>
> Virgil, *Aeneid*, trans. John Dryden

specific kinds, which we now call genres: "the heroic, lyric, tragic, comic, satiric, iambic, elegiac, pastoral."[2]

Sidney then introduces and quickly dismisses four counter-arguments: poetry is distracting, full of lies, full of fanciful ideas, and it was banished from Plato's Republic.[3] These are all refuted by a restatement of the previous case: that poetry is the highest form of learning, and is more concerned with ideal states than unthinkingly reflecting events. After a short discussion of the current state of poetry in England, Sidney closes by reasserting that poetry is the mark of virtue, and those who truly appreciate it are "most fair, most rich, most wise."[4]

Exploring the Ideas

Sidney's arguments for poetry all focus on the idea that it improves the reader by showing him ideal or heroic behavior, but in a form that is engaging and memorable. Sidney proves this first by a comparison to philosophy and history, which he argues do not teach as well, since they do not delight. It is poetry's power to produce emotion that makes it an important catalyst for changing the feelings and desires of its readers, since that emotion forces an inward re-examination in the reader that history does not. Sidney then appears to reverse his argument, providing but then dismissing four counter-arguments that poetry is untruthful or distracting. Each of these dismissals returns to the central themes established in the introductory narrative, arguing passionately yet logically that poetry is a way of discovering and emulating the ideal condition of either the individual or the state.

Poetry thus becomes a method of thought, unconstrained by reality, which can examine ideal states and perfect models of behavior. The consequence of this idea is examined at great length in the *Defence*, and is in fact the main reason Sidney gives for the necessity of poetry. He argues that, rather than being a distraction from society's needs (breeding "wanton sinfulness and lustful love"[5]), poetry teaches its readers how best to serve the common good: "Who readeth Aeneas* carrying old Anchises on his back that wisheth not it were his fortune to perform so excellent an act?"[6] Sidney's reference here is to Virgil's *Aeneid*, in which the hero Aeneas carries his father Anchises on his back as he flees the destruction of Troy on his way to becoming the ancestor of the Romans. This story became the pattern for self-sacrifice and filial duty in the Renaissance.

Sidney suggests that readers, enjoying and being moved by the texts they read, will be inspired to reproduce the acts that they find in poetry. Thus, because poets can present these heroic acts in the best possible way (that is, the most delightful and the most instructive), they are more powerful than the narrative-free disciplines of philosophy or history: "what philosopher's counsel can so readily direct ... a virtuous man in all fortunes as Aeneas in Virgil"?[7]

Language and Expression

The rhetorical style of the *Defence* is itself highly literary, concerned with using the right words in the right rhythm. The style thus links the form and content, with remarkable success. That is, the tract itself conforms to the Renaissance ideas about prosody* it sets forth, so that the ideas seem to flow without interruption, moving swiftly from point to point. It is precisely the flow of the text that gives it such rhetorical power. It is designed to carry the reader along not just with the persuasive power of its arguments, but with the wit and learned way in which they are expressed. The *Defence* conforms to its own principle that poetry (literature) should both "delight and teach";[8] it is for this reason that readers often find that they cannot get a grasp on any single one of Sidney's arguments, but instead only get a general impression of the power of poetry from the steady accumulation of ideas. The form and the content of the text work together as evidence of the delightful and instructive nature of literature, just as Sidney contends.

However, the modern reader must carefully unpick the strands of Sidney's rhetorical style in order to examine his individual arguments. Most of these arguments are rooted in Renaissance debates about the nature and value of literature. The treatise relies on knowledge not just of classical forms, but an in-depth study of the authors of Greek and Roman antiquity. While these figures would have formed part of a standard education in the early modern period, they no longer do. The modern reader is therefore often left confused and forced to rely on explanatory notes that can disrupt the flow of the text until those references become more familiar. Indeed, it may be worth initially reading the text for the broad arguments, and then a second time following up Sidney's references in more detail to better understand the nuances of his rhetoric.

NOTES

1   Philip Sidney, *The Defence of Poesy*, in *Sidney's "The Defence of Poesy" and Selected Renaissance Literary Criticism*, ed. Gavin Alexander (London: Penguin, 2004), 9.

2   Sidney, *The Defence of Poesy*, 11.

3   Plato, *Republic*, in *Classical Literary Criticism*, ed. D.A. Russell and Michael Winterbottom (Oxford: Oxford University Press, 1998).

4   Sidney, *The Defence of Poesy*, 53.

5   Sidney, *The Defence of Poesy*, 35.

6   Sidney, *The Defence of Poesy*, 23.

7   Sidney, *The Defence of Poesy*, 17.

8   Sidney, *The Defence of Poesy*, 11.

MODULE 6
SECONDARY IDEAS

KEY POINTS

- Poetry is the most perfect form of truth.
- Sidney's division of poetry into kinds became an important precedent for Renaissance understanding of poetry.
- *The Defence* is now used as a primary text, rather than as a piece of criticism.

Other Ideas

The key argument of Philip Sidney's *The Defense of Poesy* is that poetry expresses a pure truth about human nature, and encourages its readers to emulate it. This leads Sidney to three issues that, though they arise from his core ideas, are not vital to them. Most obviously, this leads him to refute Plato's assertion that poets are "far removed indeed from the truth."[1] Plato offers this assertion in his *Republic*, a thought-experiment in which he sets out the conditions for an ideally managed city. These include removing all poets, because poetry gives a false impression of real life. Sidney's refutation comes from the superordinate argument that poetry offers not reality but an ideal state, or a chance for better understanding; this idea, used as a refutation of Plato, comes originally from Aristotle's *Poetics* (a series of lectures on poetry) in which he argues that through poetry readers "come to understand something."[2]

The second theme to emerge from the key issues is the consideration of the actual practice of poetry; this is where Sidney's text is closest in form to his forebears, both contemporary and classical. This leads first to the separation of poetry into genres. Sidney separates poetry into "heroic, lyric, tragic, comic, satiric,

> ❝ [Poetry is] subdivided into sundry more special
> denominations. The most notable be the heroic, lyric,
> tragic, comic, satiric, iambic, elegiac, pastoral and
> certain others, some of these being termed according
> to the matter they deal with, some by the sorts of
> verses they liked best to write in. ❞
>
> Sidney, *Defence of Poesy*

iambic, elegiac, pastoral and certain others."[3] This division was the
first consideration of poetry by genre since Aristotle's division into
tragedy, comedy and lyric (in the *Poetics*).

Finally, the consideration of practice leads Sidney to digress into
the current state of poetry in England. He argues that, with a few
exceptions, English poetry is not living up to the ideals he outlines in
the rest of the *Defence*.

Exploring the Ideas

To both develop and refute Plato's accusation that poets are liars,
Sidney adds the point that they never claim to tell the truth in any
case: "though he recount things not true, yet because he telleth them
not for true, he lieth not."[4] Though a minor idea, and perhaps
somewhat paradoxical, the point is an important part of his overall
argument: poetry is different in both form and result from those
types of writing that are bound by events as they happened, or can
be observed; by never making a claim to truth, poetry works on a
level above the mundanity of observed events, concerned instead
with the ideal state of things, and convinces its readers to approach
that perfect state.

Allied to this broad understanding of poetry is a smaller
consideration of how to practice and critique poetry. Sidney's
extension of Aristotle's genres became a Renaissance norm, though

the period did not necessarily categorize individual poems into genres. Rather, genre was largely treated as an abstract category to be discussed as an ideal form of poetry. The *Defence* thus opened the possibility that poets might write, and so critics might consider, different types of poetry (or literature) in diverse ways. In doing so, the *Defence* laid the foundation for much modern criticism, most obviously genre-oriented criticism, and the idea of heteroglossia,* or the distinction between different forms of writing such as the epic poem and the novel, found in Bakhtin.*5

In the digression on the current state of poetry in England, Sidney breaks off from the standard rhetorical pattern, since he should move directly from the refutations to the summary; it is, though, stylistically the same as the rest of the text. Rather than the earlier examples of ideal practice drawn from Greece, the Roman Empire and Italy, Sidney directly discusses English literature for the only time in the tract. Though his classical sources do use some contemporary examples, the *Defence* extends and develops this practice and is the first sustained critical examination of current poetry in English.

Overlooked

Since its publication over 400 years ago, *The Defence of Poesy* has received sustained critical attention. Renaissance literary theory developed from Sidney's text; the Romantic period picked up many of his ideas from both prose and poetry as they reconsidered their own poetic mission; and the 20th century saw a re-examination of the *Defence* as a biographical and historical artifact. Sidney biographers returned to the *Defence*, as it is one of the few pieces of his non-fiction writing that survives.6 Therefore, very little remains in this relatively short text that has not been carefully examined, considered and reconsidered.

However, many areas of the *Defence* are neglected now because they are so intimately connected with Renaissance thought. The classical background to poetry that opens the treatise, establishing that poetry has been the main form of communication for philosophers, history writers, and theologians, is both skillful and playful; however, neither the history of thought it sketches out, nor the idea that poetry is the "first nurse" which enables the inspired poet to feed his society "afterwards of tougher knowledges," are particularly useful to scholars in those disciplines today.[7] Similarly, the digression into Sidney's contemporary poets, are primarily interesting to Renaissance scholars, rather than students of poetry in the broader sense. As such, the *Defence* tends now to be used as a piece of evidence for Renaissance ideology, or the contemporary reputation of the figures Sidney discusses.

NOTES

1   Plato, *Republic*, in *Classical Literary Criticism*, ed. D.A. Russell and Michael Winterbottom (Oxford: Oxford University Press, 1998), 47.

2   Aristotle, *Poetics*, in *Classical Literary Criticism*, 54.

3   Philip Sidney, *The Defence of Poesy*, in *Sidney's "The Defence of Poesy" and Selected Renaissance Literary Criticism*, ed. Gavin Alexander (London: Penguin, 2004), 11.

4   Sidney, *The Defence of Poesy*, 34.

5   M.M. Bakhtin, "Epic and Novel", in *The Dialogic Imagination: Four Essays*, ed. Michael Holquist (Austin: University of Texas Press, 1981).

6   Katherine Duncan-Jones, *Sir Philip Sidney: Courtier Poet* (London: Hamish Hamilton, 1991).

7   Sidney, *The Defence of Poesy*, 4.

MODULE 7
ACHIEVEMENT

KEY POINTS

- Sidney reworks attacks on poetry into a lively and passionate defense of the form.

- Though we might now call it literary criticism, the *Defence* also drew on works of philosophy, history and art.

- The classical allusions Sidney uses are less immediate for modern readers, lessening the impact of the *Defence*.

Assessing the Argument

The Defence of Poesy is unquestionably a powerful and effective argument for the power and virtue of literary endeavor. Sidney has produced a tightly argued and well-structured piece, keeping to the confines of classical rhetoric and using them to his advantage as he builds his argument. Ultimately, as a rhetorical piece, its effectiveness can only truly be judged by each individual reader, though it was popular and well-received in its time, and in the century or so that followed. Moreover, Sidney's work spurred other authors to join the debate, beginning what we now call the discipline of literary criticism (though that disciplinary boundary was not known to Sidney, nor was its creation his intent), and encouraging further investigation into the value of poetry, and the forms it might take.

Sidney reframes the attacks on poetry as a morally loose art form into a spirited defense of the ways in which it is not lies but "true doctrine" and not degenerate but "of notable stirring of courage."[1] He even reclaims Plato in defense of poets, claiming that though they were banished from his ideal commonwealth, this was only because poetry had been abused in practice, rather than because Plato wished

> **❝** I conclude therefore that he excelleth history, not only in furnishing the mind with knowledge, but in setting it forward to that which deserveth to be called and accounted good.... For who will be taught, if he be not moved with desire to be taught? **❞**
>
> Sidney, *Defence of Poesy*

to make attack on poetry itself. In doing so, Sidney raises poetry to the level of philosophy, claiming it is an authoritative way of investigating the world, and changing its audience for the better.

Achievement in Context

The Defence of Poesy was written at a time before the division of scholarship into the specialized fields with which we are familiar today.[2] Sidney himself was a poet and a scholar, a military leader and capable politician. Although we might now describe *The Defence of Poetry* as "literary criticism," it was in its contemporary moment really a rhetorical text, and so covered literature, history, philosophy, and politics, among other fields—essentially, almost everything covered by the term "humanities" today.

The text is not really a "manual" for poetry in the way that Horace's *Ars Poetica* was seen to be by Renaissance writers, although it was taken up by poets almost as soon as it was written. Nor is it entirely a guide to literary criticism in the sense of close reading as we know it today, although in its discussion of genre it is certainly an early form of critical theory. Alongside these literary applications, early readers responded to the philosophical implications of the *Defence*. The question of the truth-value of poetry had been raised in Plato's *Republic*, from which poets were banished because they were liars; Sidney's answer, that poets labor not "to tell you what is or is not, but what should or should not be," opened a critical space in which types of truth, and their relative value, could be discussed.[3]

Despite these caveats, the *Defence* was clearly a successful intervention into the debates around poetry: not only did it play a part in securing a victory for poetry against its opponents (classical and modern), it helped to establish a new genre of literary criticism. Throughout the seventeenth century, it became increasingly common for poets and writers to justify their own works (often in prefaces to the reader), and offer their thoughts on the state of poetry in general, a tradition that originated with Sidney's *Defence*.

Limitations

Much of the impact of *The Defence of Poesy* is rooted in the concerns and debates of the late Elizabethan period. Sidney's methodology is now somewhat outdated in its formality, even if the basic structure of an academic argument is much the same (introduction–evidence–conclusion). This is largely because many of the references and allusions he uses are no longer as important as they were in the Renaissance. For example, in one sentence he cites Heliodorus's* prose romance *Aethiopica*, Aeschylus's* drama *Oresteia*, Ariosto's epic *Orlando Furioso*, Xenophon's educational tract *Cyropedia* and Virgil's epic *The Aeneid*, none of which are available to the modern reader with the same immediacy and ease as they would have been for the classically educated Sidney.

Similarly, the digression towards the end of the *Defence* is largely concerned with writers who are no longer much read (with the exception of Chaucer*). For example, Spenser's* *Shepheardes Calendar* (1579) is a deliberately archaic pastoral poem in twelve parts. Despite being singled out for praise by Sidney, the text is neither well known nor easily accessible to the modern reader. The focus on "England, the mother of excellent minds" reveals a nationalistic edge to the treatise, culminating in what Shepherd calls in his useful introduction "a celebration of the limitless potential of the English tongue."[4] This naturally limits the *Defence* to an interest in the prosody of English, rather than poetry in general (in any language). Sidney rejects, for example, the "cumbersome differences of cases, genders, moods and tenses" of Romance languages.[5]

Engaging with the literary criticism of the ancient world is no longer a priority for modern scholars, except as historical texts that have influenced later writers. Much the same status is now afforded *The Defence of Poesy*: it is acknowledged as a (if not *the*) point of origin for English literary criticism, but no longer speaks to us directly. As such, it is either read for its influence on later schools of thought, especially modernism,* or for what it can tell us about Renaissance thought and the development of English poetry.[6]

NOTES

1 Philip Sidney, *The Defence of Poesy*, in *Sidney's "The Defence of Poesy" and Selected Renaissance Literary Criticism*, ed. Gavin Alexander (London: Penguin, 2004), 41.

2 Nicholas Jardine, "Epistemology of the Sciences," in *The Cambridge History of Renaissance Philosophy*, ed. Quentin Skinner and Eckhard Kessler (Cambridge: Cambridge University Press, 1988).

3 Sidney, *The Defence of Poesy*, 34.

4 Philip Sidney, *An Apology for Poetry* [1595] ed. Geoffrey Shepherd (Manchester: Manchester University Press, 2002), 41, 74.

5 Sidney, *The Defence of Poesy*, 51.

6 Michael H. Levenson, *A Genealogy of Modernism: A Study of English Literary Doctrine 1908–1922* (Cambridge: Cambridge University Press, 1984), 75.

MODULE 8
PLACE IN THE AUTHOR'S WORK

KEY POINTS

- The *Defence* is Sidney's only critical work, but it should be read alongside his poetry.
- Like all of Sidney's writing, the *Defence* was published posthumously.
- Sidney's reputation as a courtier and soldier, as well as a poet, ensured his works remained important.

Positioning

The Defence of Poesy is the only known piece of literary criticism by Sidney, and was probably composed during the 1580s, around the same time as (perhaps even slightly before) *Astrophil and Stella*. When Sidney says at the start of the *Defence* that he has "slipped into the title of a poet," he is probably referring to his own sonnet writing.[1] In this context, the *Defence* becomes not just an abstract, rhetorical defense of an art form, but a justification of the poet's own career: "Sidney's treatise established the theoretical value of poetry, and his sonnet sequence conclusively demonstrated it."[2] Sidney's literary career was interrupted by service both at court and as a diplomat overseas, before his death just a few years after composing the *Defence*, but the various works which circulated among friends, and the revisions he made to them, suggest Sidney's growing and sustained interest in the improvement of English poetry, and in particular showing it was capable of imitating, and even exceeding, great writing in other languages.

Like the *Defence*, Sidney's poetic work draws upon classical and European precedents: this includes the Petrarchan* sonnet form, but

> **❝I will give you a nearer example of myself, who (I know not by what mischance) in these my old years and idlest times having slipped into the title of a poet am provoked to say something unto you in the defense of that my unelected vocation.❞**
>
> Sidney, *The Defence of Poesy*

Sidney also tries English versions of a whole range of classical forms within the *Arcadia*. However, partly because of the differences between poetry and prose, this is generally by allusion or copying, instead of through the explicit engagement of the *Defence*.

Integration

None of Sidney's work was published (printed) within his lifetime, though it did circulate in manuscript form. Sidney's three key texts (*The Defence of Poesy*, *Arcadia*, and *Astrophil and Stella*) were all printed in the 1590s, some years after his death, from manuscripts written by Sidney. It was his literary output—the prose romance *Arcadia*, reworked by his sister, Mary Herbert,* as *The Countess of Pembroke's Arcadia* (also known as the "new" *Arcadia*), and the sonnet sequence *Astrophil and Stella*—that attracted most attention, and his *Collected Works* was a hugely popular text, frequently reprinted in the 17th century.

Sidney was best known among his contemporaries for the *Arcadia*, a prose romance with political overtones concerned with the dangers of negligent or passive government in both the family and the state. He also wrote the lengthy sonnet sequence *Astrophil and Stella*. Based on the Petrarchan sonnet sequence, both formally and in its theme of unrequited desire for an absent female, the sequence reflects Sidney's immersion in courtly life. However, it probably did not circulate widely until it was printed (in 1595, after his death) because of the potentially scandalous association of its female figure, Stella, with the married Lady Penelope Rich.*

Sidney, like his contemporaries, clearly saw the practice of poetry, and its criticism (or defense), as linked endeavors. Puttenham praised Sidney in the *Art of English Poesy* as someone who "played very prettily" with words, and it was doubtless Sidney's success as a poet that gave him the standing, and the motivation, to attempt a broader defense of the discipline.[3]

Significance

Although he was most famous for his life and his poetry, early modern authors did look to Sidney as a model for their literary criticism. As early as 1591, Sir John Harington* spoke of Sidney's desire in the *Defence* "to make poetry an art" in the preface to his translation of Ariosto's *Orlando Furioso*,[4] and nearly a century later John Dryden used Sidney as an example in the introduction to his opera *The State of Innocence*.[5]

Sidney's contention that a poet is a maker of an essential or universal truth was taken up by the Romantic* poets. Although he does not mention *The Defence of Poesy* explicitly, Shelley* is clearly drawing on this tradition when he writes in his own *Defence of Poetry* that "A poem is the very image of life expressed in its eternal truth."[6] Similarly, he adopts Sidney's argument that poetry "doth not only show the way, but giveth so sweet a prospect [view]" by stressing that "from admiring they imitated."[7] For Shelley, following Sidney, poetry is a force that, in its ability to communicate a universal truth (not subject to the tests of the newly emerging empiricism,* which was concerned only with what could be observed about the natural world), possesses the power to move its readers to imitate the actions of great men, above science, philosophy or history. In this way, Sidney's ideas on literary criticism actually outlasted the changing fashions of literature itself, finding a new voice with in a new movement.

NOTES

1   Philip Sidney, *The Defence of Poesy*, in *Sidney's "The Defence of Poesy" and Selected Renaissance Literary Criticism*, ed. Gavin Alexander (London: Penguin, 2004), 4.

2   Katherine Duncan-Jones, *Sir Philip Sidney: Courtier Poet* (London: Hamish Hamilton, 1991), 231.

3   George Puttenham, *The Art of English Poesy* (1589), in *Sidney's "The Defence of Poesy" and Selected Renaissance Literary Criticism*, ed. Gavin Alexander (London: Penguin, 2004), 170.

4   John Harington, *Orlando Furioso* (London: Richard Field, 1591), 3.

5   John Dryden, *The State of Innocence and Fall of Man: An Opera* (London: Henry Hills,1677), 11.

6   Percy Bysshe Shelley, "A Defence of Poetry," in *Essays, Letters from Abroad, Translations and Fragments*, ed. Mary Shelley (London: Lea & Blanchard, 1840), 32.

7   Sidney, *The Defence of Poesy,"* 23; Shelley, "A Defence of Poetry," 32.

SECTION 3
IMPACT

MODULE 9
THE FIRST RESPONSES

KEY POINTS

- Sidney's work helped to inaugurate a genre of poetic criticism in English.

- Sidney died before his text could receive a critical response, but some people commented on it before publication.

- Sidney's main opponents had already been vanquished, so a consensus soon grew around the value of poetry and criticism.

Criticism

Direct responses to the Philip Sidney's *Defence of Poesy* are relatively rare, though that is partly because Renaissance writers expected their readers to be up to date in their literary taste, and so spoke in general terms about the discipline, rather than providing direct references or footnotes to guide them. John Harington praises the *Defence* in his 1591 translation of Ariosto's epic poem *Orlando Furioso*, saying that for questions of the nature of poetry "I will refer you to Sir Philip's Sidney's *Apology*, who doth handle them right learnedly."[1] Much of Harington's introduction to the *Orlando Furioso* is a consideration of the power of poetry (especially in translation) and is drawn directly from Sidney's ideas on poetry, suggesting an acceptance of his ideas on the moral virtues of poetry at least among poets.

In the years following the printing of the *Defence* (both the authorized and pirated editions), a number of texts were printed which were concerned with either the moral power of poetry, or as anatomies of the specifics of poetry (rhyme, meter, genre and so forth)

> **❝**[My] meaning is plainely and *bonafide*, confessing all the abuses that can truly be obiected against some kind of Poets, to shew you what good use there is of Poetrie.**❞**
>
> John Harington, *Orlando Furioso*

in English. Though these texts did not always explicitly engage with Sidney's *Defence*, they are clearly a product of an intellectual environment that had been conceptualized in *The Defence of Poesy*. Sidney's text marks out a space, and a language, in which English poetry can be discussed, and this doubtless encouraged other authors to consider the issues it raises.

Responses

Philip Sidney died in 1586, nine years before *The Defence of Poesy* was printed (and then quickly reprinted in 1598 as part of a collected works including the *Arcadia*, revised by his sister). Between the time he first started writing the text in manuscript form (probably around 1580) and his death, it is impossible to know who either read it or how far any revisions Sidney made while writing were a response to their criticism or input.

Collaboration in the production of a text was not unusual in Renaissance England, and especially not for Sidney. He was part of a group of writers and thinkers now commonly referred to as the "Sidney circle," and it is likely Sidney consulted at least some members of this group, either in person or in writing; the manuscript of the *Defence* circulated among at least some of them while Sidney was composing it.

A version was given to his secretary, William Temple, who performed a logical analysis presumably designed to help Sidney refine the arguments to forestall criticism.[2] The manuscript must also have been seen by Sir John Harington, who calls on Sidney's text in the preface to his translation of the *Orlando Furioso*, to justify his own poetic endeavors.[3] It seems likely, though it is impossible to prove, that their responses had at least some bearing on the final text that ultimately emerged.

Conflict and Consensus

Sidney was known to his age as a version of the ideal Renaissance man. He fulfilled all of the roles available to men of his age: Sidney was a dashing traveller, a witty courtier, a poet, a tragic lover and a military commander. His *Astrophil and Stella* served as the basis for courtly narrative sonnet sequences during the peak of their popularity in the 1590s, and the *Arcadia* was quoted and adapted in literary works well into the 18th century. Given this literary influence, it is not surprising that *The Defence of Poesy* was seen as a key example of a poet writing about poetry, and was reprinted in a number of editions throughout the 16th century, often alongside his poetical works.

The *Defence* seems to have been taken up as an authoritative piece of rhetorical criticism. Despite the warnings from Puritan groups to avoid being "drawn to vanity by wanton poets," much of the anti-literary controversy of the 1580s had receded by the time it was printed, though Sidney's text, and those it inspired, helped to confirm the victory of the poets.

The two main successors to Sidney's *Defence* were Thomas Campion's* *Observations in the Art of English Poesie* and Samuel Daniel's *A Defence of Rhyme*. Campion was a musical theorist, interested in the correlation between poetic meter and musical rhythm. Campion borrows Sidney's understanding of the purpose of poetry (it "rais[es] the mind to a more high and lofty conceit"[4]), and develops the brief comments Sidney makes about rhyme ("verse being but an ornament and no cause to poetry"[5]) into a more practical understanding of how rhyme and meter might be properly deployed in poetry. Samuel

Daniel, himself a poet, notes that the intellectual environment is now ripe for his work on poetry, reporting in the introduction to his treatise on rhyme that he is "now seeing the times to promise a more regard to the present condition of our writings."[6] *The Defence of Poesy*, then, changed its intellectual field by encouraging reflections on the nature of poetry, a challenge that was met by authors who were much more concerned than Sidney with the specifics and practicalities of poetry.

NOTES

1   John Harington, *Orlando Furioso* (London: Richard Field, 1591), 3.

2   William Temple, *William Temple's Analysis of Sir Philip Sidney's Apology for Poetry: An Edition and Translation*, trans. John Webster (Binghampton, NY: MRTS, 1984).

3   John Harington, *Orlando Furioso*.

4   Thomas Campion, *Observations in the Art of English Poesie* (1602), sig. B3v.

5   Philip Sidney, *The Defence of Poesy*, in *Sidney's "The Defence of Poesy" and Selected Renaissance Literary Criticism*, ed. Gavin Alexander (London: Penguin, 2004), 12.

6   Samuel Daniel, *A Panegyric Congratulatory [and] Certain Epistles. With a Defence of Rhyme, Heretofore Written, and Now Published* (London: Edward Blount,1603), sig. G2r.

MODULE 10
THE EVOLVING DEBATE

KEY POINTS

- Sidney helped to establish a tradition of poets writing about poetry.

- The *Defence* also established a trajectory in English literary criticism of considering the moral, or social, elements of literature.

- Though Sidney is not directly quoted, his work on the effects of poetry on readers has echoes in current theory and criticism.

Uses and Problems

References to *The Defence of Poesy* are usually attempts to co-opt Sidney's status in support of the writer's argument. For example, the preacher Jasper Mayne* borrows the *Defence*'s categorization of poets as those who are truthful yet "recount of things not true" for a wittily ironic attack on false prophets, who he claims "are a far greater Poet then I have yet shown myself."[1] It is worth noting that this example comes from a sermon: Sidney's influence and authority and that of his works extended, in the 17th century, beyond the sphere of the conventionally literary into religious or historical texts, as indeed it was designed to do.

Sidney's legacy, of a poet defining his own art, lived on well into the twentieth century as writers such as T.S. Eliot* continued to reflect on the combination of sense and sound that made "great" poetry. As with Sidney, this involved a moral judgment as well as an awareness of poetic tradition dating back to antiquity; Eliot famously favored the metaphysical* poets such as Donne* and Marvell* over

> **"** But then, sir, as one excellently says in his Defence of Poesie, This is a kind of Poetry which belongs to those who lie in prose as well as those who fain in Verse. **"**
>
> Jasper Mayne, *A late printed sermon against false prophets*

the classically oriented, such as Milton.*[2] Though they did not engage with the precise content of *The Defence of Poesy*, Sidney's treatise was an important origin of a long—and ongoing—tradition of poetic self-reflection.

Schools of Thought

Sidney's executors rushed a copy of *The Defence of Poesy* to print in 1595 because a pirated edition of the manuscript was about to be published. While this shows the appetite for writings by Sidney (his long pastoral poem, *Arcadia*, was hugely popular, and Sidney himself had been something of a celebrity, famed for his courtly wit, writing, and skill as a soldier), it also perhaps demonstrates a demand for critical assessments of English literature after the publication of Puttenham's *Art of English Poesy* in 1589.[3] *The Defence of Poesy* was a seminal text in the development of literary criticism, as the first text about poetry in general, and English poetry in particular, written by a popular author. Unlike Puttenham's text, which is largely concerned with the formal qualities of poetry, Sidney argues forcefully for a moral dimension to literature, since it can both "teach and delight."[4]

The Defence of Poesy, alongside the contemporary *Art of English Poesy*, had a profound effect on the development of what we now term "Renaissance literary criticism" (the term "literary criticism" is anachronistic in this context, since it did not become current until the middle of the 18th century).[5] Thomas Campion, a musician, followed Sidney in seeing poetry as a moral force capable of "raising the mind to a more high and lofty conceit."[6] He adapted Sidney's *Defence* to think about the ways in which poetry corresponded to music; where Sidney was concerned with genre, Campion became interested in types of meter, though he divides and subdivides it in a manner reminiscent of the *Defence of Poesy*. One of the most influential writers and critics of the late 17th century, John Dryden,* justified his new type of verse (heroic drama) with reference to the same sense of poetry as moral force: "He so interweaves Truth with probable Fiction, that he puts a pleasing Fallacy upon us … to reward that virtue which has been rendered to us."[7]

In Current Scholarship

Modern academic divisions place *The Defence of Poetry* firmly within literature and literary history. It is largely referred to by critics researching the poets or literary figures it mentions, or attempting to assess the early modern view of literary production. As such, it tends to become one of a number of pieces of evidence deployed within a critical text. Rhetorical training, too, has fallen out of fashion. As such, disciplines such as law, history, philosophy and politics, which were intended to benefit from Sidney's exhortation to "teach and delight", no longer take his treatise into account at all.[8] Though Sidney probably intended his work on the ideal nature of poetry to be the most crucial part of his treatise ("I speak of the art and not the artificer"[9]), it is his own practice of poetry and rhetoric that now commands critical attention.

Literary theorists rarely engage directly with *The Defence of Poesy*, in large part because many of its ideas have been developed by a number of texts and critical schools in the 400 years since its publication. For example, the *Defence* foregrounds the intellectual engagement that poetry demands from its readers: it can "make many Cyruses,* if they will learn aright how and why that maker made him."[10] Sidney's idea that literature is important because of the effects it produces in readers (for Sidney, this largely takes the form of moral instruction delivered in a pleasurable way: to "teach and delight"[11]) is being examined once more in contemporary criticism, in what is termed the "turn to affect."[12] The "turn to affect" or "affective turn" is the increasing scholarly concern with the ways in which texts produce changes in the bodily experience of the reader, increasing (or decreasing) their willingness and ability to act. Though these critical schools do not explicitly engage with the *Defence*, the ideas it sets forward remain relevant within their systems of thought.

NOTES

1   Philip Sidney, *The Defence of Poesy*, in *Sidney's "The Defence of Poesy" and Selected Renaissance Literary Criticism*, ed. Gavin Alexander (London: Penguin, 2004), 34; Jasper Mayne, *A Late Printed Sermon against False Prophets* (1647), 30.

2   T.S. Eliot, "Milton," *Sewanee Review* 56 (1948).

3   George Puttenham, *The Art of English Poesy* (1589), in *Sidney's "The Defence of Poesy" and Selected Renaissance Literary Criticism*, ed. Gavin Alexander (London: Penguin, 2004).

4   Sidney, *The Defence of Poesy*, 10.

5   Puttenham, *The Art of English Poesy*.

6   Thomas Campion, *Observations in the Art of English Poesie*, sig. B3v.

7   John Dryden, *Of Dramatick Poesie* (1668), 19.

8   Sidney, *The Defence of Poesy*, 10.

9   Sidney, *The Defence of Poesy*, 20.

10 Sidney, *The Defence of Poesy*, 9.

11 Sidney, *The Defence of Poesy*, 10.

12 Gilles Deleuze and Felix Guattari, *A Thousand Plateaus: Capitalism and Schizophrenia, Vol. 2*, trans. Brian Massumi (London: Continuum, 2004).

MODULE 11
IMPACT AND INFLUENCE TODAY

KEY POINTS

- The *Defence* is an important part of the canon,* as both a piece of writing and the origin of a critical position.
- Sidney's assertion of moral virtue is still a key defense of the humanities today.
- Sidney's work also demonstrates an unusually thorough understanding of its literary, political, and cultural context.

Position

Philip Sidney's *The Defence of Poesy* is now widely accepted as an important part of the Renaissance canon. It is generally recognized as having had a profound effect on the development of early modern thought, not least in its status as the first sustained piece of literary criticism in English. It is also seen as an important moment in the development of classical thought along Renaissance or nationalist lines; the *Defence* is one of the earliest texts in English able to engage confidently with, and rework, the thinkers of classical antiquity.

However, it no longer attracts sustained critical attention as a text by itself. There are relatively few book-length studies of Sidney, or his *Defence of Poesy* (for instance, Katherine Duncan-Jones's* biography, now 20 years old, is still accepted as the authoritative source of Sidney scholarship[1]). Instead, the *Defence* is now primarily used as part of a wider look at Renaissance culture, as one of many supporting texts for critical enquiry into the development of early modern thought and literature.

The Defence of Poesy is universally accepted within the academy as a foundational text of English literary theory, as well as offering an

> ❝ [Both] tragedy and comedy are quite characteristically conceived by Sidney, in the *Apology for Poetry*, as warnings and lessons. This conception continues to dominate sociological theories of literature. ❞
> Stephen Greenblatt, *Renaissance Self-Fashioning*

insight into courtliness, nationalism,* and contemporary literature that is almost unrivalled in the period. However, this has involved a crucial shift: the *Defence* has itself become a primary source, discussed by literary critics and historians as a piece of textual evidence, not the theoretical text it was originally designed to be.

Interaction

While the *Defence of Poesy* remains an important work for Sidney scholars and those working on the Renaissance more broadly (both on writing by Sidney's contemporaries and on the issue of the reception of classical texts), it does not, of itself, generate significant debate. Where it is used, it is largely as a piece of literary evidence about the Renaissance, rather than a critical intervention of its own right. There are exceptions to this general rule, however. One recent study of New Formalism* argued that the *Defence* "offers one of the most detailed summations and performances of early modern formalism."[2] Though this forms part of a broader attempt to apply the structures of formalism to early modern literature, the *Defence* is particularly significant because not only does it discuss literature in a series of forms, it does so in a rhetorical style which is itself an excellent exemplar of formalist writing.

In another sense, the *Defence*'s most significant interactions are not within literary criticism, but more broadly within the humanities as a whole. Sarah Churchwell,* a professor of American literature as well as a prominent spokesperson for the humanities, has argued that "We understand ourselves and our world through the telling of stories [and] when we learn about other people, we also learn about ourselves."[3] Though Churchwell does not cite Sidney's *Defence*, its argument that readers of poetry, by learning of heroic or historical figures, "have found their hearts moved to the exercise of courtesy, liberality and especially courage" is the distant origin of Churchwell's position.[4]

The Continuing Debate

The Defence of Poesy marked the beginning of Renaissance investigations into literature. It argued that poetry could be a force for moral good, offering examples from important figures in history, or universal truths, in a delightful and entertaining fashion. Because *The Defence of Poesy* is now largely read as a historic document, rather than as a piece of current literary criticism, it does not really offer a challenge to any schools of thought. It considers contemporary issues of literature, European travel and, arguably, politics (Shepherd argues in his introduction to the *Defence* that it is a response to Sidney's perception of a "crisis in England's national identity"[5]). It is therefore an important text for the New Historicist* critical school. Using ideas developed by Stephen Greenblatt* in the early 1980s, New Historicists argue that literary texts need to be read in terms of the context that produced them.[6] By examining the complex relationship between the text and its culture, New Historicists argue that it is possible to discover the systems of power that structure a society. *The Defence of Poesy* is thus a valuable text because it is Sidney's explicit commentary on cultural and political society in Renaissance England. This is, of course, in contrast to the New Formalist position, which sees it as a piece of poetic criticism first and foremost.

New Historicism remains foundational to early modern literary studies, although with somewhat more diffuse aims than originally set out by Greenblatt—for example, New Historicist methodology underpins much of the work done on women and women's writing in the early modern period, even if that work is not directly New Historicist in nature. As such, Sidney's *Defence* is a key part of the Renaissance canon, directly or indirectly underpinning much work on early modern poetry and literary theory. Though rarely discussed in depth by itself, it is frequently used in its capacity as a standard piece of Renaissance thought, demonstrating the regard in which it is held as well as the consensus view of the *Defence* as a relatively uncontroversial or unchallenged text.

NOTES

1   Katherine Duncan-Jones, *Sir Philip Sidney: Courtier Poet* (London: Hamish Hamilton, 1991).

2   Corey McEleney and Jacqueline Wernimont, "Re-Reading for Forms in Sir Philip Sidney's *Defence of Poesy*" in *New Formalisms and Literary Theory* ed. Verena Theile and Linda Tredennick (London: Palgrave, 2013), 116-139 (116).

3   Sarah Churchwell, "Why the humanities matter", *Times Higher Education*, 14 November, 2014.

4   Philip Sidney, *The Defence of Poesy*, in *Sidney's "The Defence of Poesy" and Selected Renaissance Literary Criticism*, ed. Gavin Alexander (London: Penguin, 2004), 23.

5   Philip Sidney, *An Apology for Poetry* [1595] ed. Geoffrey Shepherd (Manchester: Manchester University Press, 2002), 13.

6   Stephen Greenblatt, *Renaissance Self-Fashioning* (Chicago: University of Chicago Press, 2005).

MODULE 12
WHERE NEXT?

KEY POINTS

* Sidney is an important writer of the Renaissance, but not directly part of popular culture today.
* His work does offer a useful insight into the "Sidney circle."
* It is valuable to students as an introduction to Sidney, as an effective piece of criticism, and as a guide for writing.

Potential

Philip Sidney's work, including *The Defence of Poesy*, remains an important part of the English canon. However, despite Sidney's profound influence (as a person and writer) on the Renaissance, neither he nor his texts have any real presence in the public consciousness today. The 400th anniversary of his death (1596/1996) and of the publication of his complete works (1598/1998) both passed with little comment. A search of major English newspapers for references to Sidney reveals how little the *Defence* is considered outside of the academy. The *Guardian* archives had only two results for *The Defence of Poesy*, both in articles about books and literary criticism, and the *Independent* and the *Telegraph* had no results whatsoever. It is safe to say that the public has little contact with the *Defence*, and would struggle to articulate the ideas it sets forward.

There is, however, a curious parallel with the context of *The Defence of Poesy* and modern debates surrounding film, television and social media. Sidney's text is, at least in part, a response to contemporary writers who argued that literature, and drama in particular, was a bad influence on its readers who were "drawn to vanity by wanton poets."[1] Today, that debate has shifted to the influence of sex or violence in

> ❝[If] you have so earth-creeping a mind that it cannot lift itself up to look to the sky of poetry ... thus much curse I must send you in behalf of all poets: that while you live, you live in love, and never get favor for lacking skill of a sonnet, and when you die, your memory die from the earth for want of an epitaph. ❞
>
> Sidney, *Defence of Poesy*

film and television programs, and the effect of new technology and social media on traditional forms of reading and writing.[2] This environment has reproduced arguments similar to *The Defence of Poesy*, with books such as the *Harry Potter* series being praised for encouraging good reading habits in children because they are sufficiently pleasurable as to promote further reading beyond the series.[3] The *Defence of Poesy* should be seen as a part of a wider debate about the purpose and value of literature (and culture more generally) extending from Aristotle to the present day.[4]

Future Directions

Studies of *The Defence of Poesy* as an object of itself, rather than in the broader context of work on Sidney's poetry or biography, are relatively rare. However, Catherine Bates's* recent book, *On Not Defending Poetry*, bucks that trend to offer an in-depth examination of the *Defence*. Bates argues that though the *Defence* has traditionally been read in a way that stresses its unity of form and purpose, it is important for scholars to "acknowledge the existence of inconsistency and irony within Sidney's text."[5]

The work is probably most important, and so most likely to generate further scholarship, as evidence of Sidney's relationship with the group of his fellow poets and intellectuals (particularly scholars of theology and politics) known as the "Sidney circle." Not least among these was his sister, Mary Herbert, Countess of Pembroke, who after Philip's death reworked his *Arcadia*, which was printed alongside the *Defence* in the 1598 collected works. The work of this group remains important as an example of a coterie,* but also as evidence of the ways in which texts were reworked, both by their authors and collaborators, before and after circulation in manuscript.[6] Because the *Defence of Poesy*, like many of Sidney's works, circulated in a number of different forms, before and after his death, it is particularly rich ground for these sorts of investigations.

Summary

The Defence of Poesy is now something of an academic curiosity. In the main, it is no longer read for its primary purpose: as a persuasive justification for poetic endeavors. Rather, it is treated as historical evidence for the intellectual culture of the late 16th century, or as a literary-biographical piece of Sidney's writing. Within both of these categories it has much to offer: it is both an excellent example of Renaissance humanist thought and writing, and a revealing insight into the intellectual workings of one of the period's great figures. *The Defence of Poesy* still has much to offer in response to this kind of historical scholarship.

Moreover, Sidney's *Defence* is a fine illustration of the effective blending of form and function. Though few scholars follow the rhetorical style as rigorously as Sidney does, the process by which he constructs his argument—setting out his topic, presenting a series of arguments and evidence, dealing with potential counter-arguments, and drawing a broad conclusion—is a superb example of how to structure a persuasive or critical piece. The fact that Sidney has done so while allying form and content (a well-written piece on how to write) gives it particular exemplary power.

Finally, while its central message about the power of poetry to move and delight may be critically outdated, the *Defence* has moved from literary criticism to literature: it is a witty, learned text that remains an enjoyable reminder of the reasons to appreciate literature.

NOTES

1   Stephen Gosson, *The School of Abuse* (London: 1579), 6.

2   Rebecca Smith, "Text Speak Does Not Affect Children's Use of Grammar: Study," *Daily Telegraph*, September 5th 2012.

3   Graeme Paton, "All Children Should Read Harry Potter Books by 11, Says Minister," Daily Telegraph, January 6th 2012.

4   Aristotle, *Poetics*, in *Classical Literary Criticism*, ed. D.A. Russell and Michael Winterbottom (Oxford: Oxford University Press, 1998).

5   Catherine Bates, *On Not Defending Poetry: Defence and Indefensibility in Sidney's 'Defence of Poetry'* (Oxford: OUP, 2017), 9.

6   Ryan J. Croft, "Sidney's Wounds: Poetic Physicality, Revision, and Remembrance in the Sidney Circle." *Sidney Journal* 31.2 (2013), 31-51.

GLOSSARY

GLOSSARY OF TERMS

Bricolage: A term developed by the French poststructuralist thinker Jacques Derrida to signify "the necessity of borrowing one's concepts," the assembling of a text from the cultural productions (literature, art, music and so on) available to the writer.

Canon: The canon is a group of works that are largely accepted as having shaped a particular culture (so one might speak of the "Western canon" or the "American canon").

Coterie: A group of people with shared interests; in literary terms, this is usually a group of like-minded poets or critics who share their works and ideas.

Courtier: Someone who served a monarch in person, often living inside (or near) a royal palace. These included close advisers (both domestic and military), entertainers, writers, clergy and administrators. Being "at court" was regarded as a great honor, and an opportunity for advancement.

Elizabethan: Belonging to the reign of Elizabeth I.

Empiricism: The theory that knowledge is based on what can be physically observed. Empiricism is usually linked to the development of physical (as opposed to philosophical, or mental) experiments in science during the seventeenth century.

Gray's Inn: One of the four 'Inns of Court' which provides training, accommodation and accreditation to barristers (lawyers) in England.

Heteroglossia: A term developed by the Russian literary theorist Mikhail Bakhtin to indicate the presence of different types of speaking found within a particular language system, for example the distinction between the rustic language of the peasants and the official language(s) of the cities.

Humanism: A collection of philosophical and moral ideas, all of which emphasize the potential of the human to develop and play a part in his or her community. Humanism in the Renaissance focused on developing the disciplines we know now as the humanities (history, politics, literature) in order to enrich life and encourage virtue. Though the term is now often used to mean secular, or anti-religious, groups, in the Renaissance many influential religious thinkers were also humanists, seeking to reconcile classical learning with scriptural values.

Humanist: An adherent of humanism, or something exemplifying the qualities of humanism.

Metaphysical Poetry: The metaphysical school of poetry is characterized by extended, unexpected or discordant metaphors and speculation on philosophical matters such as the nature of love.

Meter (poetry): The basic rhythm of lines of poetry, based on having some syllables stressed and others unstressed. The arrangement of the stressed and unstressed syllables creates the meter.

Modernism: A late 19th- and early 20th-century school that rejected the realism of art, seeking to express instead the fragmented nature of the world, and the processes by which it was understood, with a natural focus on new and challenging forms of art.

Nationalism: A political and cultural ideology that prioritizes the nation, and the idea of belonging to a nation, above all else, often in opposition to an international or global perspective.

New Formalism: A school of thought concerned with re-applying the structures and rules of particular poetic forms to writing. This is applied both to writers working today (in response to other poetic fashions which have broken down traditional forms) and scholarship on how those forms developed historically.

New Historicism: A way of reading literature which focuses on the cultural and social conditions of its creation, either to explain the work of art itself or to discover something about that context.

Pastoral: A poetic style focused on the countryside, often including shepherds and other forms of animal husbandry.

Petrarchan Sonnet: The Petrarchan (or Italian) sonnet comprises an eight-line "octet" followed by a six-line "sestet," typically in the rhyme scheme ABBAABBA CDECDE, with the octet usually establishing a problem or emotional state, and the sestet providing a resolution. The form is named after Francesco Petrarch (1304–74).

Prosody: The rhythmic aspects of prose or poetry, including stress, intonation, inflection and meter (for poetry)—that is, how literary or oral effects are created by everything except word choice.

Puritan: A term for a range of groups who believed that the church should entirely follow the scriptural examples of the Bible. They also preached against any diversion from the "pure" New Testament in day-to-day life, including frivolities such as Christmas, alcohol, and the theatre, which they saw as corrupting influences.

Renaissance: A cultural shift that took place in Europe approximately 1300–1700, and flourished in England during the 16th and early 17th centuries. Sparked by the re-discovery of texts of classical Greece and Rome, scholars across Europe revived and reconsidered ancient ideas and their modern applications.

Romanticism: A movement that placed a high value on sensory experience, especially the production of emotion. The Romantics argued that poets and artists had a special sensibility, often in affinity with nature, which could be articulated and communicated through art and literature. Key poets in this movement are William Wordsworth (1770–1850), Percy Bysshe Shelley (1792–1822) and John Keats (1795–1821).

PEOPLE MENTIONED IN THE TEXT

Aeneas is a figure from Greek and Roman mythology, a prince of Troy who travelled to Italy and founded the city from which Rome would ultimately emerge.

Aeschylus (523-456BCE) was a Greek playwright. He expanded the number of characters within tragic plays, thus enlarging the prospect of conflict between them.

Aristotle (384-22BCE) was a Greek philosopher and student of Plato. His writings covered a range of topics, including literature, history, logic, physics, ethics, and zoology.

Roger Ascham (1514-68) was a classicist and educator. He was tutor, and later adviser, to Queen Elizabeth I, and wrote a treatise on education (*The Schoolmaster*), which stressed the value of language learning and exercise as part of a rounded curriculum.

Mikhail Mikhailovich Bakhtin (1895-1975) was a Russian literary and social critic. His work focused on the forms of language in different genres of writing, as well as the social values inherent in those genres.

Catherine Bates is Professor in English at the University of Warwick. She works primarily on the courtly poetry of the sixteenth century.

Thomas Campion (1567-1620) was an English poet and musical composer. As well as songs and lyrics for court performances, his work included treatises on the ideal forms of both poetry and music.

Baldassare Castiglione (1478-1529) was an Italian courtier, diplomat and author. He is best known for his treatise *The Book of the Courtier*, an advice manual for those serving monarchs, which was popular all across Europe.

Charles I Stuart (1600-49) was king of England from 1625 until he was executed for tyranny in 1649. His attempts to dismiss Parliament and rule as an absolute monarch led to the Civil War (1642-49), and he was executed after his defeat by the Parliamentary forces.

Geoffrey Chaucer (c.1343-1400) was an English writer. He is best known for his long poem *The Canterbury Tales*, in which a group of pilgrims come together and tell stories of their lives and professions.

Sarah Churchwell (b. 1970) is professorial fellow in American literature and chair of public understanding of the humanities at the School of Advanced Study, University of London.**Cicero (106–43BCE)** was a Roman politician and lawyer. He was a leading political figure of his age, but is now largely remembered for his brilliant speeches and prose writings.

Cyrus (c.600-530BCE) was the King of Persia from 559BCE until his death. Known as 'Cyrus the Great', he incorporated most of the Middle East into his empire, supported the arts, and established a code of laws.

John Dryden (1631-1700) was a poet, dramatist, and translator. He served as Poet Laureate, and apart from his literary achievements, was notable for his ingenuity in combing dramatic forms to create the tragicomedy and the heroic drama.

John Dudley, Duke of Northumberland (1504-53) was an English nobleman and politician. He led the government for Edward VI during his minority, and was executed for trying to install Lady Jane Grey on the throne after Edward's death.

Katherine Duncan-Jones (b. 1941) is an English literary scholar. She has written on Shakespeare and Sidney, and is currently an honorary professor of English at University College, London.

T. S. Eliot (1888-1965) was an American poet and critic. He experimented with technique and style in his poetry, and his 1922 work *The Waste Land* is one of the most important and influential poetic texts of the 20th century.

Elizabeth I Tudor (1533-1603) was Queen of England from 1558-1603. Known as the "Virgin Queen," she remained unmarried in order to balance power between her rival suitors in England and on the continent. She also patronized writers and philosophers.

Stephen Gosson (1554-1624) was an English actor and anti-theatrical writer. He wrote a number of plays, but then retired to the country where he published a series of scathing attacks on the theatre as a cause of social disorder.

Stephen Greenblatt (b. 1943) is currently Cogan University Professor of the Humanities at Harvard University. His 1980 work *Renaissance Self-Fashioning* established the school of thought known as New Historicism, and his reputation as a leading scholar of the Renaissance.

Lady Jane Grey (1537-53) was the cousin of Edward VI. She was installed on the throne by John Dudley, and reigned for 9 days before being deposed and eventually executed by Mary I.

Sir John Harington (1560-1612) was an English writer and translator. His writings often touched on taboo subjects, and so he fell in and out of favor with Queen Elizabeth.

Heliodorus of Emesa (3rd century BCE) was a Greek writer. His *Aethiopica* tells the story of Chariclea, who is perceived to have been illegitimate, is forced to flee Ethiopia, and eventually falls in love with a Greek nobleman.

Mary Herbert, Countess of Pembroke (1561-1621) was an English poet, patron of the arts, and Philip Sidney's sister. She was one of the earliest major women writers in England, and also performed many chemistry experiments.

Horace (65-8BCE) was a Roman poet. He wrote a series of works in praise of the Roman emperors, as well as reflections on the art of writing.

Longinus (1st century BCE) was an anonymous figure, credited with the prose text *On the Sublime*, which deals with the aesthetics and values of poetry.

Andrew Marvell (1621-78) was an English politician and poet. He was a key figure in the school of metaphysical poetry.

Mary I Tudor (1516-58) was Queen of England from 1553-1558. She is now remembered largely for her often violent attempts to restore Roman Catholicism to England, publicly executing over 250 dissenters who objected.

Jasper Mayne (1604-72) was an English clergyman. He was a minor poet and playwright, before retiring from literature to focus on his church work and publishing sermons.

John Milton (1608-74) was an English poet (most famous for *Paradise Lost*) and a staunch supporter of the Parliamentary cause. He wrote a number of polemical pieces supporting Parliament and arguing for the establishment of a republic, including *Eikonoklastes*, which justifies the execution of a monarch.

Philip II Habsburg (1527-98) was King of Spain 1556-98, as well as ruling over Portugal, Naples, Sicily, and Milan. His rule established Spain as a dominant global power, with territories across the globe, and he made Madrid the capital of Spain.

Plato (427-347BCE) was a Greek philosopher. He helped lay the foundations of Western philosophy with his work on science, philosophy and mathematics, as well as his *Republic*, a contemplation of the ideal form of government.

George Puttenham (c.1520-90) was an English courtier. Little is known of his life, but he is credited with writing *The Arte of English Poesie*, a seminal text in poetic criticism.

Lady Penelope Rich (1563-1607) was an English noblewoman and courtier. She was considered one of the great beauties of her age, and inspired many poets and painters, including Philip Sidney.

Percy Bysshe Shelley (1792-1822) was an English poet. He was one of the leading figures of the Romantic movement.

Edmund Spenser (1552-99) was a noted poet and a colonial administrator in Ireland. He became famous for the pastoral (country) poem *The Shepheardes Calendar* (1579), and the allegorical epic *The Faerie Queene* (1596).

Virgil (70-19BCE) was a Roman epic poet. His most famous work is the *Aeneid*, the story of the travels of Aeneas, and the origins of Rome.

Xenophon (4th century BCE) was a Greek poet and soldier. His *Cyropedia* offers a (probably) fictionalized account of the education of Cyrus, King of Persia.

WORKS CITED

WORKS CITED

Aristotle. *Poetics*. Translated by M.E. Hubbard. In *Classical Literary Criticism*, edited by D.A. Russell and Michael Winterbottom, 51–90. Oxford: Oxford University Press, 1998.

Ascham, Roger. *The Schoolmaster.* London: John Daye, 1570.

Bakhtin, M.M. "Epic and Novel." Translated by Caryl Emerson and Michael Holquist. In *The Dialogic Imagination: Four Essays*, edited by Michael Holquist, 3–40. Austin: University of Texas Press, 1981.

Bates, Catherine. *On Not Defending Poetry: Defence and Indefensibility in Sidney's 'Defence of Poetry'*. Oxford: OUP, 2017.

Campion, Thomas. *Observations in the Art of English Poesie*. 1602.

Carew, Richard. *Survey of Cornwall*. 1602.

Castiglione, Baldassare. *The Courtier of Count Baldessar Castilio Divided into Four Books*. Translated by Thomas Hoby. 1561.

Churchwell, Sarah. "Why the humanities matter." *Times Higher Education*, 14 November, 2014.

Cicero, Marcus Tullius. *On the Ideal Orator*. Translated by James M. May and Jakob Wisse. Oxford: Oxford University Press, 2001.

Croft, Ryan J. "Sidney's Wounds: Poetic Physicality, Revision, and Remembrance in the Sidney Circle." *Sidney Journal* 31.2 (2013), 31-51.

Daniel, Samuel. *A Panegyric Congratulatory [and] Certain Epistles. With a Defence of Rhyme, Heretofore Written, and Now Published*. 1603.

Deleuze, Gilles and Felix Guattari. *A Thousand Plateaus: Capitalism and Schizophrenia, Vol. 2*. Translated by Brian Massumi. London: Continuum, 2004.

Dryden, John. *Of Dramatick Poesie*. 1668.

The State of Innocence and Fall of Man: An Opera. 1677.

Duncan-Jones, Katherine. *Sir Philip Sidney: Courtier Poet*. London: Hamish Hamilton, 1991.

Eliot, T.S. "Milton." *Sewanee Review* 56 (1948): 185–209.

Fowler, Alastair. "The Formation of Genres in the Renaissance and After." *New Literary History* 34.2 (2003) 185-200.

Gosson, Stephen. *The School of Abuse*. London: 1579.

Greenblatt, Stephen. *Renaissance Self-Fashioning*. 2nd ed. Chicago: University of Chicago Press, 2005.

Harington, John. *Orlando Furioso*. London: Richard Field, 1591.

Horace. *Ars Poetica*. Translated by D.A. Russell. In *Classical Literary Criticism*, edited by D.A. Russell and Michael Winterbottom, 98–110. Oxford: Oxford University Press, 1998.

Jardine, Nicholas. "Epistemology of the Sciences." In *The Cambridge History of Renaissance Philosophy*, edited by Quentin Skinner and Eckhard Kessler, 685–712. Cambridge: Cambridge University Press, 1988.

Levenson, Michael H. *A Genealogy of Modernism: A Study of English Literary Doctrine 1908–1922*. Cambridge: Cambridge University Press, 1984.

Mayne, Jasper. *A Late Printed Sermon against False Prophets*. 1647.

McEleney, Corey, and Jacqueline Wernimont. "Re-Reading for Forms in Sir Philip Sidney's *Defence of Poesy.*" In *New Formalisms and Literary Theory,* edited by Verena Theile and Linda Tredennick (London: Palgrave, 2013), 116-139.

Milton, John. *Eikonoklastes* (1649), in *Complete Prose of John Milton*, edited by Merritt Y. Hughes, 6 vols. New Haven: Yale University Press, 1962.

Paton, Graeme. "All Children Should Read Harry Potter Books by 11, Says Minister." *Daily Telegraph*, 6 January 2012.

Plato. *Republic*. Translated by D.A. Russell. In *Classical Literary Criticism*, edited by D.A. Russell and Michael Winterbottom, 14–50. Oxford: Oxford University Press, 1998.

Puttenham, George. *The Art of English Poesy* (1589), in *Sidney's "The Defence of Poesy" and Selected Renaissance Literary Criticism*, edited by Gavin Alexander. London: Penguin, 2004.

Shelley, Percy Bysshe. "A Defence of Poetry." In *Essays, Letters from Abroad, Translations and Fragments*, edited by Mary Shelley, 25–62. London: Lea & Blanchard, 1840.

Sidney, Philip. *An Apology for Poetry*. Manchester: Manchester University Press, 2002.

"*The Defence of Poesy*" (1595). In *Sidney's 'the Defence of Poesy' and Selected Renaissance Literary Criticism*, edited by Gavin Alexander, 1–54. London: Penguin Classics, 2004.

Smith, Rebecca. "Text Speak Does Not Affect Children's Use of Grammar: Study." *Daily Telegraph*, 5 September 2012.

Stubbs, George. *The Anatomy of Abuses*. 1583.

Temple, William. *William Temple's Analysis of Sir Philip Sidney's Apology for Poetry: An Edition and Translation*. Translated by John Webster. Binghampton, NY: MRTS, 1984.

Wilson, Thomas. *The Art of Rhetoric*. 1553.

THE MACAT LIBRARY
BY DISCIPLINE

AFRICANA STUDIES

Chinua Achebe's *An Image of Africa: Racism in Conrad's Heart of Darkness*
W. E. B. Du Bois's *The Souls of Black Folk*
Zora Neale Huston's *Characteristics of Negro Expression*
Martin Luther King Jr's *Why We Can't Wait*
Toni Morrison's *Playing in the Dark: Whiteness in the American Literary Imagination*

ANTHROPOLOGY

Arjun Appadurai's *Modernity at Large: Cultural Dimensions of Globalisation*
Philippe Ariès's *Centuries of Childhood*
Franz Boas's *Race, Language and Culture*
Kim Chan & Renée Mauborgne's *Blue Ocean Strategy*
Jared Diamond's *Guns, Germs & Steel: the Fate of Human Societies*
Jared Diamond's *Collapse: How Societies Choose to Fail or Survive*
E. E. Evans-Pritchard's *Witchcraft, Oracles and Magic Among the Azande*
James Ferguson's *The Anti-Politics Machine*
Clifford Geertz's *The Interpretation of Cultures*
David Graeber's *Debt: the First 5000 Years*
Karen Ho's *Liquidated: An Ethnography of Wall Street*
Geert Hofstede's *Culture's Consequences: Comparing Values, Behaviors, Institutes and Organizations across Nations*
Claude Lévi-Strauss's *Structural Anthropology*
Jay Macleod's *Ain't No Makin' It: Aspirations and Attainment in a Low-Income Neighborhood*
Saba Mahmood's *The Politics of Piety: The Islamic Revival and the Feminist Subject*
Marcel Mauss's *The Gift*

BUSINESS

Jean Lave & Etienne Wenger's *Situated Learning*
Theodore Levitt's *Marketing Myopia*
Burton G. Malkiel's *A Random Walk Down Wall Street*
Douglas McGregor's *The Human Side of Enterprise*
Michael Porter's *Competitive Strategy: Creating and Sustaining Superior Performance*
John Kotter's *Leading Change*
C. K. Prahalad & Gary Hamel's *The Core Competence of the Corporation*

CRIMINOLOGY

Michelle Alexander's *The New Jim Crow: Mass Incarceration in the Age of Colorblindness*
Michael R. Gottfredson & Travis Hirschi's *A General Theory of Crime*
Richard Herrnstein & Charles A. Murray's *The Bell Curve: Intelligence and Class Structure in American Life*
Elizabeth Loftus's *Eyewitness Testimony*
Jay Macleod's *Ain't No Makin' It: Aspirations and Attainment in a Low-Income Neighborhood*
Philip Zimbardo's *The Lucifer Effect*

ECONOMICS

Janet Abu-Lughod's *Before European Hegemony*
Ha-Joon Chang's *Kicking Away the Ladder*
David Brion Davis's *The Problem of Slavery in the Age of Revolution*
Milton Friedman's *The Role of Monetary Policy*
Milton Friedman's *Capitalism and Freedom*
David Graeber's *Debt: the First 5000 Years*
Friedrich Hayek's *The Road to Serfdom*
Karen Ho's *Liquidated: An Ethnography of Wall Street*

John Maynard Keynes's *The General Theory of Employment, Interest and Money*
Charles P. Kindleberger's *Manias, Panics and Crashes*
Robert Lucas's *Why Doesn't Capital Flow from Rich to Poor Countries?*
Burton G. Malkiel's *A Random Walk Down Wall Street*
Thomas Robert Malthus's *An Essay on the Principle of Population*
Karl Marx's *Capital*
Thomas Piketty's *Capital in the Twenty-First Century*
Amartya Sen's *Development as Freedom*
Adam Smith's *The Wealth of Nations*
Nassim Nicholas Taleb's *The Black Swan: The Impact of the Highly Improbable*
Amos Tversky's & Daniel Kahneman's *Judgment under Uncertainty: Heuristics and Biases*
Mahbub Ul Haq's *Reflections on Human Development*
Max Weber's *The Protestant Ethic and the Spirit of Capitalism*

FEMINISM AND GENDER STUDIES

Judith Butler's *Gender Trouble*
Simone De Beauvoir's *The Second Sex*
Michel Foucault's *History of Sexuality*
Betty Friedan's *The Feminine Mystique*
Saba Mahmood's *The Politics of Piety: The Islamic Revival and the Feminist Subject*
Joan Wallach Scott's *Gender and the Politics of History*
Mary Wollstonecraft's *A Vindication of the Rights of Woman*
Virginia Woolf's *A Room of One's Own*

GEOGRAPHY

The Brundtland Report's *Our Common Future*
Rachel Carson's *Silent Spring*
Charles Darwin's *On the Origin of Species*
James Ferguson's *The Anti-Politics Machine*
Jane Jacobs's *The Death and Life of Great American Cities*
James Lovelock's *Gaia: A New Look at Life on Earth*
Amartya Sen's *Development as Freedom*
Mathis Wackernagel & William Rees's *Our Ecological Footprint*

HISTORY

Janet Abu-Lughod's *Before European Hegemony*
Benedict Anderson's *Imagined Communities*
Bernard Bailyn's *The Ideological Origins of the American Revolution*
Hanna Batatu's *The Old Social Classes And The Revolutionary Movements Of Iraq*
Christopher Browning's *Ordinary Men: Reserve Police Batallion 101 and the Final Solution in Poland*
Edmund Burke's *Reflections on the Revolution in France*
William Cronon's *Nature's Metropolis: Chicago And The Great West*
Alfred W. Crosby's *The Columbian Exchange*
Hamid Dabashi's *Iran: A People Interrupted*
David Brion Davis's *The Problem of Slavery in the Age of Revolution*
Nathalie Zemon Davis's *The Return of Martin Guerre*
Jared Diamond's *Guns, Germs & Steel: the Fate of Human Societies*
Frank Dikotter's *Mao's Great Famine*
John W Dower's *War Without Mercy: Race And Power In The Pacific War*
W. E. B. Du Bois's *The Souls of Black Folk*
Richard J. Evans's *In Defence of History*
Lucien Febvre's *The Problem of Unbelief in the 16th Century*
Sheila Fitzpatrick's *Everyday Stalinism*

Eric Foner's *Reconstruction: America's Unfinished Revolution, 1863-1877*
Michel Foucault's *Discipline and Punish*
Michel Foucault's *History of Sexuality*
Francis Fukuyama's *The End of History and the Last Man*
John Lewis Gaddis's *We Now Know: Rethinking Cold War History*
Ernest Gellner's *Nations and Nationalism*
Eugene Genovese's *Roll, Jordan, Roll: The World the Slaves Made*
Carlo Ginzburg's *The Night Battles*
Daniel Goldhagen's *Hitler's Willing Executioners*
Jack Goldstone's *Revolution and Rebellion in the Early Modern World*
Antonio Gramsci's *The Prison Notebooks*
Alexander Hamilton, John Jay & James Madison's *The Federalist Papers*
Christopher Hill's *The World Turned Upside Down*
Carole Hillenbrand's *The Crusades: Islamic Perspectives*
Thomas Hobbes's *Leviathan*
Eric Hobsbawm's *The Age Of Revolution*
John A. Hobson's *Imperialism: A Study*
Albert Hourani's *History of the Arab Peoples*
Samuel P. Huntington's *The Clash of Civilizations and the Remaking of World Order*
C. L. R. James's *The Black Jacobins*
Tony Judt's *Postwar: A History of Europe Since 1945*
Ernst Kantorowicz's *The King's Two Bodies: A Study in Medieval Political Theology*
Paul Kennedy's *The Rise and Fall of the Great Powers*
Ian Kershaw's *The "Hitler Myth": Image and Reality in the Third Reich*
John Maynard Keynes's *The General Theory of Employment, Interest and Money*
Charles P. Kindleberger's *Manias, Panics and Crashes*
Martin Luther King Jr's *Why We Can't Wait*
Henry Kissinger's *World Order: Reflections on the Character of Nations and the Course of History*
Thomas Kuhn's *The Structure of Scientific Revolutions*
Georges Lefebvre's *The Coming of the French Revolution*
John Locke's *Two Treatises of Government*
Niccolò Machiavelli's *The Prince*
Thomas Robert Malthus's *An Essay on the Principle of Population*
Mahmood Mamdani's *Citizen and Subject: Contemporary Africa And The Legacy Of Late Colonialism*
Karl Marx's *Capital*
Stanley Milgram's *Obedience to Authority*
John Stuart Mill's *On Liberty*
Thomas Paine's *Common Sense*
Thomas Paine's *Rights of Man*
Geoffrey Parker's *Global Crisis: War, Climate Change and Catastrophe in the Seventeenth Century*
Jonathan Riley-Smith's *The First Crusade and the Idea of Crusading*
Jean-Jacques Rousseau's *The Social Contract*
Joan Wallach Scott's *Gender and the Politics of History*
Theda Skocpol's *States and Social Revolutions*
Adam Smith's *The Wealth of Nations*
Timothy Snyder's *Bloodlands: Europe Between Hitler and Stalin*
Sun Tzu's *The Art of War*
Keith Thomas's *Religion and the Decline of Magic*
Thucydides's *The History of the Peloponnesian War*
Frederick Jackson Turner's *The Significance of the Frontier in American History*
Odd Arne Westad's *The Global Cold War: Third World Interventions And The Making Of Our Times*

LITERATURE

Chinua Achebe's *An Image of Africa: Racism in Conrad's Heart of Darkness*
Roland Barthes's *Mythologies*
Homi K. Bhabha's *The Location of Culture*
Judith Butler's *Gender Trouble*
Simone De Beauvoir's *The Second Sex*
Ferdinand De Saussure's *Course in General Linguistics*
T. S. Eliot's *The Sacred Wood: Essays on Poetry and Criticism*
Zora Neale Huston's *Characteristics of Negro Expression*
Toni Morrison's *Playing in the Dark: Whiteness in the American Literary Imagination*
Edward Said's *Orientalism*
Gayatri Chakravorty Spivak's *Can the Subaltern Speak?*
Mary Wollstonecraft's *A Vindication of the Rights of Women*
Virginia Woolf's *A Room of One's Own*

PHILOSOPHY

Elizabeth Anscombe's *Modern Moral Philosophy*
Hannah Arendt's *The Human Condition*
Aristotle's *Metaphysics*
Aristotle's *Nicomachean Ethics*
Edmund Gettier's *Is Justified True Belief Knowledge?*
Georg Wilhelm Friedrich Hegel's *Phenomenology of Spirit*
David Hume's *Dialogues Concerning Natural Religion*
David Hume's *The Enquiry for Human Understanding*
Immanuel Kant's *Religion within the Boundaries of Mere Reason*
Immanuel Kant's *Critique of Pure Reason*
Søren Kierkegaard's *The Sickness Unto Death*
Søren Kierkegaard's *Fear and Trembling*
C. S. Lewis's *The Abolition of Man*
Alasdair MacIntyre's *After Virtue*
Marcus Aurelius's *Meditations*
Friedrich Nietzsche's *On the Genealogy of Morality*
Friedrich Nietzsche's *Beyond Good and Evil*
Plato's *Republic*
Plato's *Symposium*
Jean-Jacques Rousseau's *The Social Contract*
Gilbert Ryle's *The Concept of Mind*
Baruch Spinoza's *Ethics*
Sun Tzu's *The Art of War*
Ludwig Wittgenstein's *Philosophical Investigations*

POLITICS

Benedict Anderson's *Imagined Communities*
Aristotle's *Politics*
Bernard Bailyn's *The Ideological Origins of the American Revolution*
Edmund Burke's *Reflections on the Revolution in France*
John C. Calhoun's *A Disquisition on Government*
Ha-Joon Chang's *Kicking Away the Ladder*
Hamid Dabashi's *Iran: A People Interrupted*
Hamid Dabashi's *Theology of Discontent: The Ideological Foundation of the Islamic Revolution in Iran*
Robert Dahl's *Democracy and its Critics*
Robert Dahl's *Who Governs?*
David Brion Davis's *The Problem of Slavery in the Age of Revolution*

Alexis De Tocqueville's *Democracy in America*
James Ferguson's *The Anti-Politics Machine*
Frank Dikotter's *Mao's Great Famine*
Sheila Fitzpatrick's *Everyday Stalinism*
Eric Foner's *Reconstruction: America's Unfinished Revolution, 1863-1877*
Milton Friedman's *Capitalism and Freedom*
Francis Fukuyama's *The End of History and the Last Man*
John Lewis Gaddis's *We Now Know: Rethinking Cold War History*
Ernest Gellner's *Nations and Nationalism*
David Graeber's *Debt: the First 5000 Years*
Antonio Gramsci's *The Prison Notebooks*
Alexander Hamilton, John Jay & James Madison's *The Federalist Papers*
Friedrich Hayek's *The Road to Serfdom*
Christopher Hill's *The World Turned Upside Down*
Thomas Hobbes's *Leviathan*
John A. Hobson's *Imperialism: A Study*
Samuel P. Huntington's *The Clash of Civilizations and the Remaking of World Order*
Tony Judt's *Postwar: A History of Europe Since 1945*
David C. Kang's *China Rising: Peace, Power and Order in East Asia*
Paul Kennedy's *The Rise and Fall of Great Powers*
Robert Keohane's *After Hegemony*
Martin Luther King Jr.'s *Why We Can't Wait*
Henry Kissinger's *World Order: Reflections on the Character of Nations and the Course of History*
John Locke's *Two Treatises of Government*
Niccolò Machiavelli's *The Prince*
Thomas Robert Malthus's *An Essay on the Principle of Population*
Mahmood Mamdani's *Citizen and Subject: Contemporary Africa And The Legacy Of Late Colonialism*
Karl Marx's *Capital*
John Stuart Mill's *On Liberty*
John Stuart Mill's *Utilitarianism*
Hans Morgenthau's *Politics Among Nations*
Thomas Paine's *Common Sense*
Thomas Paine's *Rights of Man*
Thomas Piketty's *Capital in the Twenty-First Century*
Robert D. Putman's *Bowling Alone*
John Rawls's *Theory of Justice*
Jean-Jacques Rousseau's *The Social Contract*
Theda Skocpol's *States and Social Revolutions*
Adam Smith's *The Wealth of Nations*
Sun Tzu's *The Art of War*
Henry David Thoreau's *Civil Disobedience*
Thucydides's *The History of the Peloponnesian War*
Kenneth Waltz's *Theory of International Politics*
Max Weber's *Politics as a Vocation*
Odd Arne Westad's *The Global Cold War: Third World Interventions And The Making Of Our Times*

POSTCOLONIAL STUDIES

Roland Barthes's *Mythologies*
Frantz Fanon's *Black Skin, White Masks*
Homi K. Bhabha's *The Location of Culture*
Gustavo Gutiérrez's *A Theology of Liberation*
Edward Said's *Orientalism*
Gayatri Chakravorty Spivak's *Can the Subaltern Speak?*

PSYCHOLOGY

Gordon Allport's *The Nature of Prejudice*
Alan Baddeley & Graham Hitch's *Aggression: A Social Learning Analysis*
Albert Bandura's *Aggression: A Social Learning Analysis*
Leon Festinger's *A Theory of Cognitive Dissonance*
Sigmund Freud's *The Interpretation of Dreams*
Betty Friedan's *The Feminine Mystique*
Michael R. Gottfredson & Travis Hirschi's *A General Theory of Crime*
Eric Hoffer's *The True Believer: Thoughts on the Nature of Mass Movements*
William James's *Principles of Psychology*
Elizabeth Loftus's *Eyewitness Testimony*
A. H. Maslow's *A Theory of Human Motivation*
Stanley Milgram's *Obedience to Authority*
Steven Pinker's *The Better Angels of Our Nature*
Oliver Sacks's *The Man Who Mistook His Wife For a Hat*
Richard Thaler & Cass Sunstein's *Nudge: Improving Decisions About Health, Wealth and Happiness*
Amos Tversky's *Judgment under Uncertainty: Heuristics and Biases*
Philip Zimbardo's *The Lucifer Effect*

SCIENCE

Rachel Carson's *Silent Spring*
William Cronon's *Nature's Metropolis: Chicago And The Great West*
Alfred W. Crosby's *The Columbian Exchange*
Charles Darwin's *On the Origin of Species*
Richard Dawkin's *The Selfish Gene*
Thomas Kuhn's *The Structure of Scientific Revolutions*
Geoffrey Parker's *Global Crisis: War, Climate Change and Catastrophe in the Seventeenth Century*
Mathis Wackernagel & William Rees's *Our Ecological Footprint*

SOCIOLOGY

Michelle Alexander's *The New Jim Crow: Mass Incarceration in the Age of Colorblindness*
Gordon Allport's *The Nature of Prejudice*
Albert Bandura's *Aggression: A Social Learning Analysis*
Hanna Batatu's *The Old Social Classes And The Revolutionary Movements Of Iraq*
Ha-Joon Chang's *Kicking Away the Ladder*
W. E. B. Du Bois's *The Souls of Black Folk*
Émile Durkheim's *On Suicide*
Frantz Fanon's *Black Skin, White Masks*
Frantz Fanon's *The Wretched of the Earth*
Eric Foner's *Reconstruction: America's Unfinished Revolution, 1863-1877*
Eugene Genovese's *Roll, Jordan, Roll: The World the Slaves Made*
Jack Goldstone's *Revolution and Rebellion in the Early Modern World*
Antonio Gramsci's *The Prison Notebooks*
Richard Herrnstein & Charles A Murray's *The Bell Curve: Intelligence and Class Structure in American Life*
Eric Hoffer's *The True Believer: Thoughts on the Nature of Mass Movements*
Jane Jacobs's *The Death and Life of Great American Cities*
Robert Lucas's *Why Doesn't Capital Flow from Rich to Poor Countries?*
Jay Macleod's *Ain't No Makin' It: Aspirations and Attainment in a Low Income Neighborhood*
Elaine May's *Homeward Bound: American Families in the Cold War Era*
Douglas McGregor's *The Human Side of Enterprise*
C. Wright Mills's *The Sociological Imagination*

The Macat Library By Discipline

Thomas Piketty's *Capital in the Twenty-First Century*
Robert D. Putman's *Bowling Alone*
David Riesman's *The Lonely Crowd: A Study of the Changing American Character*
Edward Said's *Orientalism*
Joan Wallach Scott's *Gender and the Politics of History*
Theda Skocpol's *States and Social Revolutions*
Max Weber's *The Protestant Ethic and the Spirit of Capitalism*

THEOLOGY

Augustine's *Confessions*
Benedict's *Rule of St Benedict*
Gustavo Gutiérrez's *A Theology of Liberation*
Carole Hillenbrand's *The Crusades: Islamic Perspectives*
David Hume's *Dialogues Concerning Natural Religion*
Immanuel Kant's *Religion within the Boundaries of Mere Reason*
Ernst Kantorowicz's *The King's Two Bodies: A Study in Medieval Political Theology*
Søren Kierkegaard's *The Sickness Unto Death*
C. S. Lewis's *The Abolition of Man*
Saba Mahmood's *The Politics of Piety: The Islamic Revival and the Feminist Subject*
Baruch Spinoza's *Ethics*
Keith Thomas's *Religion and the Decline of Magic*

Macat Disciplines

Access the greatest ideas and thinkers across entire disciplines, including

FEMINISM, GENDER AND QUEER STUDIES

Simone De Beauvoir's
The Second Sex

Michel Foucault's
History of Sexuality

Betty Friedan's
The Feminine Mystique

Saba Mahmood's
The Politics of Piety: The Islamic Revival and the Feminist Subject

Joan Wallach Scott's
Gender and the Politics of History

Mary Wollstonecraft's
A Vindication of the Rights of Woman

Virginia Woolf's
A Room of One's Own

Judith Butler's
Gender Trouble

 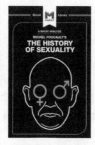  

Macat analyses are available from all good bookshops and libraries.

Access hundreds of analyses through one, multimedia tool.
Join free for one month **library.macat.com**

Macat Disciplines

Access the greatest ideas and thinkers across entire disciplines, including

CRIMINOLOGY

Michelle Alexander's
*The New Jim Crow:
Mass Incarceration in the
Age of Colorblindness*

**Michael R. Gottfredson
& Travis Hirschi's**
A General Theory of Crime

Elizabeth Loftus's
Eyewitness Testimony

**Richard Herrnstein
& Charles A. Murray's**
*The Bell Curve: Intelligence and
Class Structure in American Life*

Jay Macleod's
*Ain't No Makin' It:
Aspirations and Attainment in a
Low-Income Neighborhood*

Philip Zimbardo's
The Lucifer Effect

Macat analyses are available from all good bookshops and libraries.

Access hundreds of analyses through one, multimedia tool.
Join free for one month **library.macat.com**

Macat Disciplines

Access the greatest ideas and thinkers across entire disciplines, including

GLOBALIZATION

Arjun Appadurai's, *Modernity at Large: Cultural Dimensions of Globalisation*

James Ferguson's, *The Anti-Politics Machine*

Geert Hofstede's, *Culture's Consequences*

Amartya Sen's, *Development as Freedom*

Macat Pairs

Analyse historical and modern issues from opposite sides of an argument.
Pairs include:

HOW TO RUN AN ECONOMY

John Maynard Keynes's
The General Theory OF Employment, Interest and Money

Classical economics suggests that market economies are self-correcting in times of recession or depression, and tend toward full employment and output. But English economist John Maynard Keynes disagrees.

In his ground-breaking 1936 study *The General Theory*, Keynes argues that traditional economics has misunderstood the causes of unemployment. Employment is not determined by the price of labor; it is directly linked to demand. Keynes believes market economies are by nature unstable, and so require government intervention. Spurred on by the social catastrophe of the Great Depression of the 1930s, he sets out to revolutionize the way the world thinks

Milton Friedman's
The Role of Monetary Policy

Friedman's 1968 paper changed the course of economic theory. In just 17 pages, he demolished existing theory and outlined an effective alternate monetary policy designed to secure 'high employment, stable prices and rapid growth.'

Friedman demonstrated that monetary policy plays a vital role in broader economic stability and argued that economists got their monetary policy wrong in the 1950s and 1960s by misunderstanding the relationship between inflation and unemployment. Previous generations of economists had believed that governments could permanently decrease unemployment by permitting inflation—and vice versa. Friedman's most original contribution was to show that this supposed trade-off is an illusion that only works in the short term.

Macat analyses are available from all good bookshops and libraries.

Access hundreds of analyses through one, multimedia tool.
Join free for one month **library.macat.com**

Macat Disciplines

*Access the greatest ideas and thinkers
across entire disciplines, including*

THE FUTURE OF DEMOCRACY

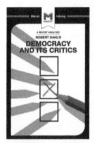

Robert A. Dahl's, *Democracy and Its Critics*
Robert A. Dahl's, *Who Governs?*
Alexis De Toqueville's, *Democracy in America*
Niccolò Machiavelli's, *The Prince*
John Stuart Mill's, *On Liberty*
Robert D. Putnam's, *Bowling Alone*
Jean-Jacques Rousseau's, *The Social Contract*
Henry David Thoreau's, *Civil Disobedience*

Macat Pairs

Analyse historical and modern issues from opposite sides of an argument. Pairs include:

RACE AND IDENTITY

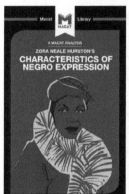

Zora Neale Hurston's
Characteristics of Negro Expression

Using material collected on anthropological expeditions to the South, Zora Neale Hurston explains how expression in African American culture in the early twentieth century departs from the art of white America. At the time, African American art was often criticized for copying white culture. For Hurston, this criticism misunderstood how art works. European tradition views art as something fixed. But Hurston describes a creative process that is alive, ever-changing, and largely improvisational. She maintains that African American art works through a process called 'mimicry'—where an imitated object or verbal pattern, for example, is reshaped and altered until it becomes something new, novel—and worthy of attention.

Frantz Fanon's
Black Skin, White Masks

Black Skin, White Masks offers a radical analysis of the psychological effects of colonization on the colonized.

Fanon witnessed the effects of colonization first hand both in his birthplace, Martinique, and again later in life when he worked as a psychiatrist in another French colony, Algeria. His text is uncompromising in form and argument. He dissects the dehumanizing effects of colonialism, arguing that it destroys the native sense of identity, forcing people to adapt to an alien set of values—including a core belief that they are inferior. This results in deep psychological trauma.

Fanon's work played a pivotal role in the civil rights movements of the 1960s.

Macat analyses are available from all good bookshops and libraries.

Access hundreds of analyses through one, multimedia tool.
Join free for one month **library.macat.com**

Macat Pairs

Analyse historical and modern issues from opposite sides of an argument. Pairs include:

INTERNATIONAL RELATIONS IN THE 21ˢᵀ CENTURY

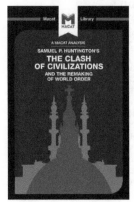

Samuel P. Huntington's
The Clash of Civilisations

In his highly influential 1996 book, Huntington offers a vision of a post-Cold War world in which conflict takes place not between competing ideologies but between cultures. The worst clash, he argues, will be between the Islamic world and the West: the West's arrogance and belief that its culture is a "gift" to the world will come into conflict with Islam's obstinacy and concern that its culture is under attack from a morally decadent "other."

Clash inspired much debate between different political schools of thought. But its greatest impact came in helping define American foreign policy in the wake of the 2001 terrorist attacks in New York and Washington.

Francis Fukuyama's
The End of History and the Last Man

Published in 1992, *The End of History and the Last Man* argues that capitalist democracy is the final destination for all societies. Fukuyama believed democracy triumphed during the Cold War because it lacks the "fundamental contradictions" inherent in communism and satisfies our yearning for freedom and equality. Democracy therefore marks the endpoint in the evolution of ideology, and so the "end of history." There will still be "events," but no fundamental change in ideology.